OVERSEAS REPRESENTATION AND SERVICES FOR FEDERAL DOMESTIC AGENCIES

by Robert E. Elder

CARNEGIE ENDOWMENT FOR INTERNATIONAL PEACE

1965

OVERSEAS REPRESENTATION AND SERVICES FOR FEDERAL DOMESTIC AGENCIES

FOREIGN AFFAIRS PERSONNEL STUDIES

FOREWORD

DURING THE COURSE OF THE DELIBERATIONS of the Committee on Foreign Affairs Personnel in 1961 and 1962, the staff of the Committee conducted a number of investigations and surveys to assist the Committee in reaching its conclusions. Although most of the salient findings of these studies were carefully considered by the Committee, they could not be prepared for publication in time to accompany the Committee report, *Personnel for the New Diplomacy,* which was presented to the Secretary of State and published in December 1962. The Committee believed that much of the material gathered for its own use would be of continuing interest and value to practitioners and students in the field of foreign affairs administration. Accordingly, the staff was requested to proceed with the development of selected monographs for publication.

Since the Committee was formally disbanded in January 1963, its responsibility for the staff studies ended with that request. The preparation for publication of the six studies, of which the present monograph by Robert E. Elder is the second, has been undertaken by the authors themselves, with the help and guidance of Professor Frederick C. Mosher, who was the Committee's Staff Director. I wish to record my appreciation and that of my colleagues on the Committee to them and to the Carnegie Endowment for International Peace, which sponsored the Committee itself and is publishing these monographs.

CHRISTIAN A. HERTER

v

PREFACE

THE CONDUCT OF FOREIGN POLICY in a world of rapid change has become a matter of crucial importance to all Americans. Of continuing—and growing—concern are the character and quality of foreign affairs personnel and of the personnel systems designed to put the right people in the right places in diplomatic, informational, and foreign assistance activities. Sharing this concern with the Secretary of State and other senior officials responsible for foreign affairs personnel, the Carnegie Endowment in 1961 responded enthusiastically to a request that it sponsor a new independent study of personnel needs and of the ways to meet them. This was the genesis of the Committee on Foreign Affairs Personnel, which received financial support from the Ford Foundation and the Rockefeller Brothers Fund, as well as from the Carnegie Endowment.

With former Secretary of State Christian A. Herter as Chairman, the Committee carried out a survey of the selection, education and training, and career development of United States foreign affairs personnel. Concentrating on the needs of the Department of State, the Agency for International Development, and the United States Information Agency, the Committee attempted to appraise the nation's personnel needs in the field of foreign affairs for the next decade. It focused upon measures needed to increase the government's ability to find and make maximum use of professional personnel with the essential skills.

In support of this survey, wide-ranging and intensive research was needed. The Committee's professional staff and consultants delved into the history of foreign services, of American agencies, and of other committees on foreign affairs personnel. They gathered pertinent statistics and examined personnel procedures at home and in overseas assignments. At meetings of the full Committee or its subcommittees, in interviews with members of the Committee or its staff, or in writing, more than one thousand foreign affairs officials and experts contributed their knowledge and views. All this provided the basis on which the Committee prepared its report and offered its recommendations for improvements that would require administrative or legislative action.

The Endowment, believing that the Committee's objectives would be furthered by making the results of staff studies available to the many scholars who are studying problems related to those of the Committee's inquiry, was more than willing to undertake the responsibility for publishing these monographs. I hope and believe they will contribute to knowledge about, and better understanding of, a crucial and too often slighted requirement for the successful conduct of foreign relations—first-class men and women, carefully recruited, well trained, and in the right jobs.

It is a privilege and a pleasure to express, on behalf of the Endowment, lasting gratitude to Mr. Herter and the other distinguished gentlemen who served on the Committee, to the staff and consultants, and to the Ford Foundation and the Rockefeller Brothers Fund.

JOSEPH E. JOHNSON, *President*
Carnegie Endowment for International Peace

CONTENTS

ix

INTRODUCTION

AS A CONSEQUENCE OF THE BURGEONING INTERESTS and responsibilities of the United States government at home and abroad over the past quarter century, it has become increasingly difficult to distinguish clearly between foreign policy matters and matters of domestic concern. It is commonplace today to observe that there is no "water's edge" by which to compartmentalize our overseas undertakings; they are woven into the fabric of virtually all our national issues and programs. The historic structure of the federal departments and agencies, however, reflects such a division, and the accommodation of domestic-foreign considerations with the existing and evolving structure has been, and will undoubtedly continue to be, a persistent problem of public administration. For a century and a half, the Department of State was the primary and almost sole agency—except on military matters and in time of war—that was officially concerned with affairs beyond the water line. Even in wartime the division was not as sharp as it appeared, since the Department did perform a number of functions overseas that were of interest to other agencies of the government and sometimes were done at their request.

Since the passage of the Rogers Act in 1924, the overseas arm of the Department of State has been officially known as the Foreign Service of the United States, a designation clearly suggesting that the State Department would continue as the principal repository of overseas responsibilities and would perform such activities abroad as the other agencies of the government might require in addition to its more traditional diplomatic and consular functions. During the 1920s and 1930s, nonetheless, there was a gradual increase in the overseas activities by other departments of government, notably the departments of Agriculture, Commerce, Interior, and the Treasury. Agricultural and commercial activities abroad were consolidated within the regular Foreign Service in 1939, but World War II brought an enlargement of direct overseas programs of other agencies, as well as a proliferation of new functions in foreign affairs, some of which resulted in the creation of new agencies. Another wave of integration under the Foreign Service occurred in the early postwar years, but this principle could not contain the tremendous expansion of American overseas interests. The organizational and personal responses to these needs were expressed in a series of improvisations that followed no consistent design. Some programs were set up as independent agencies with their own overseas personnel programs; some were set up within, or eventually were moved into, the Department of State; others maintained their home base in another agency of the government but utilized the State Department's overseas facilities and personnel; some operated at home and abroad within their own organization, outside the Department of State.

These widely varying organizational arrangements, modified over the last fifteen years by shifts from one scheme to another, have produced today's perplexing picture. This picture may perhaps be clarified by classifying the agencies into three broad categories. It should be borne in mind, however, that there is wide variation within each:

(1) The military agencies and certain others, such as intelligence, whose primary concern is national security.

(2) Civil agencies whose primary responsibilities are in overseas matters (Department of State, Agency for International Development, United States Information Agency, Disarmament Agency, Peace Corps).

(3) Civil agencies whose primary responsibilities are in domestic affairs in the United States but which are concerned in varying ways and degrees with overseas and foreign programs.

The Committee on Foreign Affairs Personnel, which carried on most of its investigations during 1962, focused its attention upon the three largest agencies in the second category, that is, the civil foreign affairs agencies. It could hardly overlook, however, the other categories especially insofar as they were related to the personnel problems of the agencies in the second category. The third category was especially pertinent because several of these agencies utilize the personnel of the Foreign Service and all of them depend in some degree upon the overseas facilities and assistance of the Department. Furthermore, in some fields the technical assistance programs of the Agency for International Development rely heavily upon professional specialists furnished or detailed by primarily domestic agencies of the government.

The problems of overseas programs of the domestic agencies became a matter of special interest to the Committee because of developments during the course of its studies. In the first place, a number of new types of such programs were being considered, and there were some questions about the personnel arrangements vis-à-vis the Foreign Service system. Secondly, pressures were growing during the year to separate from the Foreign Service some of the older services that had previously been staffed through the Foreign Service system. In fact, a bill to remove the commercial officers from the Service and establish a separate Foreign Commerce Service under the Department of Commerce had been introduced and passed in the Senate (but not in the House). Thirdly, the Departments of State and Commerce had drawn up an agreement that contemplated continuance of the commercial functions in the Foreign Service but that provided a formal vehicle for greatly increased Commerce participation in personnel matters affecting commercial officers.

In order to provide a better basis for understanding and for judgment on these and related questions, the Committee asked Professor Robert Elder to prepare a study of the overseas activities and the personnel arrangements of the domestic agencies with major involvements abroad. His survey and the alternative proposals he presented for handling the problems were very useful to the Committee and its staff in reaching the recommendation that ultimately appeared in the Committee's report.[1] Professor Elder later amplified his study for the purposes of this monograph. The particular value of the study perhaps derives from the fact that it brings together information about the diverse activities that American agencies are involved in overseas in addition to the well-known and traditional responsibilities. It also serves to point up the variety and complexities of organizational and personnel problems attendant upon their conduct. Nowhere else have these programs been so catalogued and analyzed.

The average reader is apt to find confusing the situations described in this report. Little pattern appears in the tangled web of activities and relationships described. This may be traced partly to the episodes in recent history which have brought about the wide variety of pro-

---

[1] The Committee's recommendation appears as Appendix A of this monograph.

grams and systems. This reflects in part the divergent pressures and interests existing in our volatile and pluralistic democracy and the responses to these interests of both the legislative and executive branches of the government. It also mirrors the uncertain but rapidly changing shape of the world beyond our borders.

The underlying problem, however, is perhaps the very "nature of the beast." There is a duality of interest of at least two different agencies of government that appears entirely legitimate and indeed inevitable. The Department of State and its overseas service are held primarily responsible for the development and execution of United States foreign policy. Other departments and agencies in such fields as agriculture, labor, and atomic energy are responsible for conducting programs in their respective fields both at home and abroad. Few if any of these programs can be carried on abroad without influencing our international relations and without affecting our foreign policy in some degree. The programs can hardly be handled within the simpler precepts and caveats of administrative management. Effort has been made in the past to distinguish between these programs on the basis of their primacy of concern—whether foreign policy or domestic program. Professor Elder discusses the distinctions at greater length. As he shows, the demarcation is not a solid line but a gray zone of fluctuating and uncertain boundaries. Such is the nature of the problem.

ROBERT E. ELDER is Professor of Political Science at Colgate University. Before he joined the staff of the Committee on Foreign Affairs Personnel as a consultant, he helped draft The Brookings Institution study on *The Formulation and Administration of United States Foreign Policy,* prepared in 1959 for the Senate Foreign Relations Committee and published in 1960. Professor Elder has also written *The Policy Machine: The Department of State and American Foreign Policy,* published by Syracuse University Press in 1960, and *The Foreign Leader Program: Operations in the United States,* published by The Brookings Institution in 1961. At present, he is studying the organization and work of the United States Information Agency.

Frederick C. Mosher
Professor, University of California, Berkeley

March 1964

1 | BACKGROUND

THIS STUDY CONCERNS THE OVERSEAS INTERESTS of federal domestic agencies and the means by which they are, or might be, staffed. It deals with attache services, which have traditionally performed reporting, negotiating, and representational duties in specialized, functional fields related to the needs of domestic affairs agencies, and with personnel programs that support the more clearly overseas extensions of domestic agency activities. In considering what the relationship of overseas personnel activities might be to the Civil Service, the Foreign Service of the United States, or other personnel structures, it is necessary to review the many different personnel practices now utilized by the government in meeting the needs of the federal domestic agencies.

Underlying the relatively narrow focus of the study is a search for rational and workable personnel policies and practices that will help to solve three interlocking needs which have arisen as a result of competitive staffing or organizational requirements and which threaten the successful administration and conduct of overseas programs of the United States government:

1. The need for personnel for overseas duty with different and sometimes deeper specializations than have hitherto been found in the United States Foreign Service, without unduly sacrificing their preparation for overseas service in order to meet the special requirements of work abroad;

2. The need to adjust United States government policies so that they will contribute to a greater synthesis and positive interaction between United States foreign and domestic policies—a responsibility only recently recognized as essential to national and world security; and

3. The need to achieve a greater central control for implementing United States policy in individual countries and an assurance of adequate centralization or coordination in Washington for the formulation of foreign policy and of domestic policy that might have foreign affairs impact.

The desirability of adjusting government institutions to meet these needs is accepted as a premise. While it is apparent that the field of personnel management is only one facet of the adjustment problem, the organization of personnel should be a help, not a hindrance, to the adjustment.

In moving toward some accommodation to immediate requirements in the personnel field, policies are called for which are not only presently acceptable but which will not preclude further adaptation in the future. Past personnel practices and experiences have already limited the choice of personnel policies practical for the present.

The Rogers Act of 1924 created the Foreign Service of the United States by an amalgamation of the separate Diplomatic and Consular Services. Because it was taken for granted during the 1920s that the responsibilities of the Foreign Service should be of the traditional diplomatic and consular nature, pressures for more specialized information in the economic field led to Congressional establishment of separate overseas services for several domestic agencies. Thus, Congress authorized the creation of a Foreign Commercial Service in 1927, a Foreign Agricultural Service in 1930, and in 1935 gave the Bureau of Mines of the Department of Interior authorization for overseas representation, which led to the sending abroad of several minerals specialists. During the 1930s the Department of the Treasury sent representatives overseas on an ad hoc basis to resolve specific problems and established regular representation abroad in 1939.

During the depression of the 1930s, world-wide tariff barriers were erected so that overseas trade promotion activities were as much the concern of governments—the special clientele of the Foreign Service—as of private merchants with whom the domestic agency overseas services had expanded contacts. Problems of coordinating efforts of the Foreign Service to increase trade with the projects of the other separate services eventually led to the transfer of the overseas personnel and activities of the Departments of Commerce and Agriculture back to the Department of State and the Foreign Service on July 1,

2

1939, under the Reorganization Act No. 2 of 1939. In 1943, the small number of minerals specialists who had been sent abroad by the Bureau of Mines were also integrated into the Foreign Service. Although some Foreign Service officers resented the transfer of these so-called economic experts into their elite corps of diplomatic and consular generalists, others were equally apprehensive about the Treasury Department's decision, in 1939 (under its authority to use the proceeds from the Exchange Stabilization Fund), to send financial experts to major foreign capitals.

How well the somewhat unified Foreign Service of 1939 would have worked was never put to a proper test, for the outbreak of World War II brought about the creation of a host of wartime agencies with separate representation abroad. The overseas relationships of the United States agencies during this period were said to have been chaotic; the leadership and authority of the Department of State and the Foreign Service abroad were seriously impaired.

The Foreign Service Act of 1946 took into account the interests of the major domestic departments then concerned with overseas affairs—Agriculture, Commerce, and Labor. These departments were given representation on the Board of the Foreign Service. The Act was intended to establish a system of overseas representation, administered under the Department of State but serving the needs abroad of most United States agencies; it provided for appropriate specialists in the Foreign Service along with generalists. Only the Treasury Department continued to operate its small separate personnel system.

However, exigencies of the cold war, and growing dissatisfaction of the Departments of Agriculture, Commerce, and Labor with the job the State Department and the Foreign Service were doing as their agents, militated against further progress toward a unified Foreign Service. Under pressure from domestic agricultural interests, Congress re-established in 1954 the Foreign Agricultural Service, which maintained independent attaches overseas.

During the 1950s United States interests overseas expanded and along with them the personnel systems required to service the new activities. As of June 30, 1961, there were 31,883 United States citizens employed abroad. These were assisted by 94,675 citizens of the various countries, known as locals.

Most government employees overseas served in personnel systems of the major civil foreign affairs agencies—the Department of State, the Agency for International Development (AID), the United States Information Agency (USIA), and the Peace Corps—or those of the military and intelligence services. Of the total number of government personnel employed abroad, twenty federal domestic affairs agencies in 1961 employed only 1,671 citizens, or 5.24 per cent, and 1,314 foreign nationals, or 1.38 per cent.

VARIETY OF PRESENT ARRANGEMENTS

In many instances the domestic affairs agencies are serviced by the foreign affairs agencies. For example, labor attaches and labor reporting officers of the Foreign Service of the United States handle tasks for the Department of Labor. On the other hand, certain overseas duties of the foreign affairs agencies are performed by personnel acquired from domestic affairs agencies. Thus, employees of the Bureau of Reclamation of the Department of Interior may either be transferred for service to AID, with the right to return to the Bureau after the job has been accomplished, or perform a service for AID while remaining on the personnel rolls of the Bureau and being paid by it out of funds appropriated to AID.

Some of the domestic affairs agencies have legislative authorization to assume certain international responsibilities. The Department of Commerce, for example, has primary responsibility for promoting the expansion of United States trade with foreign countries. Most of the employees performing this task overseas, however, serve in the Foreign Service of the United States. By contrast, other domestic affairs agencies have no authorization to be overseas except for domestic purposes. Thus, employees of the National Institutes of Health help negotiate contracts with foreign governments and private institutions for the conduct of research by foreign nationals that must be justified as being of benefit to the domestic interests of the United States. Yet, it cannot be denied that such research furthers the development of the recipient nation, and therefore has a long-range foreign affairs impact.

The nature of and legislative bases for the overseas staffing of the principal foreign affairs agencies (USIA, AID, the Department of State, and others) vary widely. USIA and AID—both leading foreign affairs agencies—have no legislative authorized foreign services in the same sense as the Department of State. But the Department of Agriculture, one of the so-called domestic agencies, has a legislatively established Foreign Agricultural Service. The foregoing examples are only a few of the existing contradictions.

To point out such contradictions or apparent inconsistencies is not to call for their immediate elimination. The hand of the past usually rests heavily on human institutions and cannot be easily laid aside. In meeting overseas responsibilities, the United States government has utilized a variety of personnel systems that have been modified and made partially uniform over the years. But the systems have not

4

yet been objectively reorganized to meet new needs. In the uneasy years of transition, perhaps more could not be asked. It is probable that the time has not yet come for any total reorganization, total compatibility, or total unification of the personnel systems for United States overseas activities. This does not mean that the government cannot effect a limited reordering of the personnel systems.

At present, only two of the twenty domestic agencies maintain what are clearly accepted as attache services separate from the Foreign Service of the United States—the Department of Agriculture and the Department of the Treasury—and even these utilize many of the administrative services provided at overseas posts by the Foreign Service. There are currently strong centrifugal tendencies among the domestic agencies to increase the number of separate attache or other foreign services overseas, and there is counterpressure to place all or most domestic agency employees abroad under personnel systems controlled by the foreign affairs agencies.

DEFINITIONS

In general, most of the overseas personnel in the programs surveyed in this study can be classified either as performing one or more attache-type function or performing services that are essentially overseas extensions of federal domestic agencies. As will become evident after description and analysis of the programs, the classifications are much less clear-cut than would first appear. In fact, some personnel classified as attaches perform tasks that tend to be overseas extensions of domestic functions, while others not considered attaches actually handle attache-type services.

Attaches in all government systems are considered to be members of the diplomatic staff of a mission. According to Article 3 of the Vienna Convention on Diplomatic Relations, adopted by the United Nations Conference on Diplomatic Intercourse and Immunities on April 14, 1961,

> 1. The functions of a diplomatic mission consist, *inter alia,* in:
>
>   *a.* representing the sending State in the receiving State;
>
>   *b.* protecting in the receiving State the interests of the sending State and of its nationals, within the limits permitted by international law;
>
>   *c.* negotiating with the Government of the receiving State;
>
>   *d.* ascertaining by all lawful means conditions and developments in the receiving State, and reporting thereon to the Government of the sending State;
>
>   *e.* promoting friendly relations between the sending State and

the receiving State, and developing their economic, cultural and scientific relations.

2. Nothing in the present Convention shall be construed as preventing the performance of consular functions by a diplomatic mission.

William Barnes and John H. Morgan state: "The title of 'attaché' is usually assigned to an officer who performs a specialized function. There are, for example, labor, agricultural, and commercial attachés. An officer of the armed services who is assigned to a diplomatic mission is given the title of Army Attaché, Naval Attaché, or Air Attaché." [1]

Personnel who only perform tasks that represent an overseas extension of activities of a federal domestic agency usually are not considered members of the diplomatic staff of a mission. Performing such functions are those who carry out regulation and control or research activities at posts abroad essentially for domestic purposes,[2] and who administrate or operate an overseas project primarily servicing a program of a federal domestic agency.[3]

PERSONNEL SYSTEMS

Many of the persons abroad who serve the overseas interests of federal domestic agencies are members of the Foreign Service of the United States. Some attaches have had long careers as regular Foreign Service officers specializing in the overseas activities of a particular domestic agency. This is true of many commercial and labor attaches. Others have been appointed as members of the Foreign Service Reserve and may at some future date either enter the Foreign Service or return to Civil Service appointments in the United States with the agency whose interests they had served abroad. Minerals, fisheries, and civil aviation attaches are normally in this category. Clerical and some administrative personnel assisting attaches may be members of the Foreign Service Staff corps. Foreign Service officers and Foreign Service Staff personnel serve in a career service, with their rank determined by promotions in the service rather than by the jobs to which they are assigned. They are committed to accept assignments anywhere in the world, subject to the needs of the Service.

Most personnel abroad serving the domestic agencies are members

---

[1] *The Foreign Service of the United States: Origins, Development, and Functions* (Washington: Dept. of State, Historical Office, Bureau of Public Affairs, 1961), pp. 308-309.

[2] For example, customs agents of the Bureau of Customs and research entomologists of the Agricultural Research Service.

[3] For example, station managers are technical representatives of the National Aeronautics and Space Administration.

of the Civil Service. These individuals often do not hold attache-type positions but perform functions relating to the extension of a domestic agency program overseas. There are important exceptions to this rule, notably agricultural attaches and Treasury representatives. These individuals have normally entered the Civil Service expecting to serve primarily in the United States but have later been selected for overseas duty. In many instances, they expect to serve for a limited period overseas and then return to continue their careers in the United States. Their pay and grade schedules are determined by the classification of the job to which they are assigned. They do not carry a personal rank and are not subject to assignment overseas without their consent.

In addition to the Foreign Service and the Civil Service, there are other personnel systems that maintain personnel overseas to service domestic agencies, such as the Public Health Service Commissioned Officers Corps. In many respects, its career system is similar to that of the Foreign Service. The personnel systems for Atomic Energy Commission scientific representatives and for Federal Bureau of Investigation legal attaches are considered to be "excepted services," that is, outside the Civil Service. While they employ many devices that stem from the Civil Service personnel system, they are under the direct control of their individual agencies, and not subject to regular Civil Service limitations.

This study is based on a survey of twenty-three programs and personnel systems of ten major domestic affairs agencies with substantial and widespread interests in overseas programs. Specifically excluded from consideration are personnel activities of the federal domestic agencies in support of programs of AID, USIA, the Central Intelligence Agency, the Department of Defense, the Peace Corps, and international organizations of which the United States is a member.[4] Nonetheless, the more than 500 professional or officer-level personnel staffed by the domestic agencies directly and the approximately 250 Foreign Service or Foreign Service Reserve officers serving their interests overseas represent a high proportion of all such United States government employees working abroad.

The personnel serving in the various programs studied ranged widely in number. For example, there were 149 commercial specialists in the Foreign Service or Foreign Service Reserve serving overseas but only one social welfare attache; there were approximately 125 employees of the Foreign Agricultural Service who had been or were members of the Agricultural Attache Service but there were only three fisheries attaches. More typical in number were the 66 labor attaches, 28 Department of Agriculture employees performing regu-

---

[4] The relations of domestic agencies with AID are outlined briefly in Appendix C.

lation and control functions abroad, 14 professional employees overseas for the Atomic Energy Commission, 8 minerals attaches servicing the Bureau of Mines of the Department of Interior, 35 special agents of the FBI serving as legal attaches, 15 station managers and special representatives of the National Aeronautics and Space Administration, and 16 Treasury representatives. Two proposed programs of the Department of Health, Education, and Welfare were studied but these did not, of course, have any personnel overseas.

Most of the material for this study was drawn from 85 interviews, conducted during May, June, and August 1962, with personnel in the following departments and agencies: Agriculture; Atomic Energy Commission; Commerce; Federal Aviation Agency; Health, Education, and Welfare; Interior; Justice; Labor; National Aeronautics and Space Administration; and Treasury. Additional interviews were held in the Department of State, the Bureau of the Budget, and the Civil Service Commission. Most of the interviews were scheduled with individuals but in some instances were held with groups of from three to ten agency representatives.

The first major section of the study—following two tables that attempt to categorize programs by functions and by personnel systems—is a description of personnel programs tentatively designed as attache-type. A second section concerns programs tentatively classified as non-attache-type. A third section is an analysis of the existing personnel systems, indicating some of the principal problems that must be resolved to improve the representation of federal domestic agencies overseas. A final section considers possible alternative relationships of attache services to the Foreign Service of the United States.

TABLE 1

ANALYSIS OF AGENCY PROGRAMS SURVEYED
Classified According to Types of Function

Agencies	Reporting, Negotiating, Representational, and Trade Promotion Function	Regulation and Control Activities	Research Activities	Other Programs
AGRICULTURE	Foreign Agricultural Service (Agricultural Attache Service)	Agricultural Research Service (Regulation and Control)	Agricultural Research Service (American Research Abroad) Agricultural Research Service (P.L. 480 Foreign Research)	
ATOMIC ENERGY COMMISSION	Division of International Affairs (AEC Scientific Representatives)			
COMMERCE	Assistant Secretary for Domestic and International Affairs (Commercial Specialization Program)			
FEDERAL AVIATION AGENCY	International Aviation Service (Civil Aviation Attaches)	Flight Standards Service (Aviation Safety Officers, Facilities Flight Inspection)		
HEALTH, EDUCATION, AND WELFARE	Office of Education (Proposed Educational Attaches) Welfare Administration (Social Welfare Attaches) Vocational Rehabilitation Administration (Proposed Vocational Rehabilitation Attaches)*	Bureau of Medical Services (Division of Foreign Quarantine)	National Institutes of Health (P.L. 480 Foreign Research)†	
INTERIOR	Bureau of Mines (Minerals Attaches) Bureau of Commercial Fisheries (Fisheries Attaches)			
JUSTICE		Federal Bureau of Investigation (Legal Attaches) Immigration and Naturalization Service (Immigration Officers)		
LABOR	Bureau of International Labor Affairs (Labor Attaches)			
NASA				Office of International Programs (Station Managers and Technical Representatives)
TREASURY	Office of International Affairs (Treasury Representatives)	Bureau of Customs (Customs Agents and Representatives) Bureau of Narcotics (Narcotics Agents) Internal Revenue Service (Revenue Service Representatives)		

* The Vocational Rehabilitation Administration's proposed attaches are placed under the "Reporting, Negotiating, Representational, and Trade Promotion Function" in spite of the fact that they might also perform functions related to the "Research Activities" category. This is a good example of the problem of categorizing multiple-function programs.

† It should be noted that functions given by the National Institutes of Health for their overseas personnel included others in addition to the administration of "Research Activities" of the P.L. 480 program, some of which might be considered as reporting, negotiating, or representation under the "Reporting, Negotiating, Representational, and Trade Promotion Function" category.

TABLE 2

ANALYSIS OF AGENCY PROGRAMS SURVEYED
Classified According to Types of Personnel Systems

Agencies	Foreign Service	Civil Service	Other Services
AGRICULTURE		Foreign Agricultural Service (Agricultural Attache Service) Agricultural Research Service (Regulation and Control) Agricultural Research Service (American Research Abroad) Agricultural Research Service (P.L. 480 Foreign Research)	
ATOMIC ENERGY COMMISSION			Division of International Affairs (AEC Scientific Representatives)
COMMERCE	Commercial Specialization Program		
FEDERAL AVIATION AGENCY	Civil Aviation Attaches	Flight Standards Service (Aviation Safety Officers, Facilities Flight Inspection)	
HEALTH, EDUCATION, AND WELFARE	Proposed Education Attaches Social Welfare Attaches Proposed Vocational Rehabilitation Attaches	National Institutes of Health (P.L. 480 Foreign Research)*	Bureau of Medical Services (Division of Foreign Quarantine)
INTERIOR	Minerals Attaches Fisheries Attaches		
JUSTICE		Immigration and Naturalization Service (Immigration Officers)	Federal Bureau of Investigation (Legal Attaches)
LABOR	Labor Attaches		
NASA		Office of International Programs (Station Managers and Technical Representatives)	
TREASURY		Office of International Affairs (Treasury Representatives) Bureau of Customs (Customs Agents and Representatives) Bureau of Narcotics (Narcotics Agents) Internal Revenue Service (Revenue Service Representatives)	

* Note that the National Institutes of Health P.L. 480 foreign research program and other of their overseas programs are also administered by members of the Public Health Service Commissioned Officer Corps which would fall under the "Other Service" category.

II ATTACHE-TYPE PROGRAMS

PROGRAMS TO BE DESCRIBED under this heading are grouped together more for convenience of organization and because they have some similarities than because they are identical. Any attempt to categorize programs by the functions their personnel perform must be somewhat imprecise, for personnel often support programs with more than one purpose. Nonetheless, attache-type programs may be defined briefly as those in which the staff perform reporting, negotiating, and representational functions and which may include trade promotion or other specialized activities. Most of the programs discussed here will fall within this definition, although some functions of the proposed vocational rehabilitation attache program might be considered as outside the attache field.

Programs with functions that appear to be largely of an attache-type are discussed under three headings: (1) Independent programs, which are those whose personnel are not members of the Foreign Service of the United States. They include: the agricultural attaches of the Foreign Agriculture Service of the Department of Agriculture; the Treasury representatives of the Department of the Treasury; and the Atomic Energy Commission scientific representatives. (2) Related programs, which are those whose personnel are members of the Foreign Service or the Foreign Service Reserve. They include: the Commercial Specialist Program with a special relationship to the Department of Commerce; the labor attaches with a special relationship to the Department of Labor; the civil aviation attaches with a special relationship to the Federal Aviation Agency; and the minerals and fisheries attaches with a special relationship to the Department of Interior. (3) Listed separately under proposed and new programs are: projected educational attache and vocational rehabilitation attache programs of the Department of Health, Education, and Welfare, and the recently reinstituted welfare attache program of the same Department.

INDEPENDENT PROGRAMS

Department of Agriculture: The Foreign Agricultural Service (Agricultural Attache Service)

Functions. Agricultural attaches are the chief suppliers of world agricultural "economic intelligence," reporting on marketing opportunities abroad and on foreign production that might compete with American commodities. They estimate export possibilities and import requirements in the countries of assignment. Under a new emphasis, the attaches "actively" seek markets and market opportunities for United States agricultural products. They endeavor to remove trade barriers, assist United States exporters in making contacts with foreign importers, keep close watch on the reception of United States products by foreign consumers, and suggest improvements to increase the preference for American farm commodities. They also promote the surplus utilization program for farm commodities under P.L. 480.[1] They service American farmers and professional agriculturalists visiting abroad and report on new agricultural research developments or on the outbreak of animal diseases and plant pests. They are under the administrative supervision of the ambassador and are considered members of the "country team." They do not normally advise foreign countries on how to improve their agricultural research and practices.

Developments, Size, and Qualifications. The Foreign Agricultural Service was established as an agency of the Department of Agriculture in 1930 and functioned as a separate overseas service with some responsibilities for market development until 1939. At that time, the threat of war shifted emphasis from trade promotion to trade control, and the functions of the Foreign Agricultural Service were transferred by Executive Order to the Foreign Service of the United States

---

[1] *The Agricultural Trade Development and Assistance Act of 1954,* 83rd Congress, 2nd Sess. (S.2475), Chapter 469.

12

under the Secretary of State. An Office of Foreign Agricultural Relations was established in 1939 to assist the Secretary of Agriculture in maintaining working relations with the Department of State and the Foreign Service. It helped to select agricultural personnel for the Foreign Service and took part in the assignment of agricultural officers.

Agricultural officials believe that the Department of State assumed responsibility for the agricultural attache function in good faith but lacked the resources to do the job. As time passed, the Department of Agriculture found that too many Foreign Service "generalists" were being assigned to agricultural work. Department of State control of dispatches to and from the field limited Department of Agriculture contact with the agricultural attaches. When the Department wanted to establish a new post abroad, the State Department sometimes allowed it only on the condition that the post be filled by a person that the State Department had available at the time. Agricultural officials felt more and more remote from the attaches and believed that the State Department had all the "say-so."

In the 1940s there was a great demand abroad for agricultural commodities, and control of these commodities continued to be more important than promotion of their sale. But in the years following World War II, agricultural surpluses began piling up in the United States. The new Republican administration in 1953 wanted to avoid domestic controls as a means of resolving the agricultural surplus problem and thought marketing abroad offered an obvious outlet for such surpluses. In the judgment of the Agriculture Department, however, the Foreign Service was not geared to this type of work. The Department of State budget had been cut sharply, and Agriculture believed that the Foreign Service had reduced agricultural attache activities "disproportionately" in response to the cut. The eighty men formerly assigned to perform such duties were reduced to fifty, and junior officers with no agricultural training or background were increasingly assigned to agricultural responsibilities. Farm organizations and agricultural trade groups were also unhappy with the way the Foreign Service was handling marketing activities and took their troubles to sympathetic members of Congress.

When domestic pressures built up in Congress for the re-establishment of a separate Foreign Agricultural Service, the Department of Agriculture took the position that it was not going to "lock horns" with its own people when the State Department had been ignoring its wishes. Title VI of P.L. 690, passed on August 28, 1954, gave the Secretary of Agriculture the right to appoint attaches abroad for the purpose of developing foreign markets for American farm products, and for acquiring and disseminating economic intelligence data on foreign demand for and competition with American farm products.

A number of career commodity specialists stationed in Washington review all the reports and material received from attaches, and from Foreign Service officers. These trained specialists interpret and evaluate the contents of the reports. It is by this careful analysis that final estimates are made on world agricultural production, programs, and development.

In the United States the Foreign Agricultural Service has initiated forty market development programs which are being carried on with the cooperation of trade and farm groups such as the National Renderers Association, Great Plains Wheat, Soybean Council and Cotton Council International. Over 400 market development projects in fifty countries are also being actively carried out in an effort to promote the sales and exports of United States farm products. This joint effort between the Foreign Agricultural Service and trade and farm groups is one of the most significant developments since the attaches were returned to the Department of Agriculture in 1954.

By 1962, the level of Agriculture's overseas staff had risen again to 80-85 officers and 35-40 locally recruited staff making a total of 270, including foreign clerical and professional employees. This does not include the Washington staff that supports the overseas program in the Foreign Agricultural Service. All told, the Service employed 693 Americans at home and abroad in June 1962, and 137 foreign nationals at overseas posts. The Foreign Service still provides all administrative services overseas for which it is reimbursed by the Foreign Agricultural Service. Agricultural attaches are accorded diplomatic status and are entitled to most of the benefits applicable to the Foreign Service, but serve under Civil Service appointment and compensation systems.

The Foreign Agricultural Service operates on an independent budget which it must obtain annually from the Appropriation Committees of the House of Representatives and the Senate respectively. It receives over 5,000 agricultural reports every year from its agricultural attaches. These reports come directly to the Department of Agriculture and are reproduced on facilities operated by the Foreign Agricultural Service. Some of the reports are distributed through the regional offices of the Agricultural Marketing Service and the Agricultural Stabilization and Conservation Service: they go directly to trade sources which have particular interest in either commodity or regional developments. A whole series of publications based on these reports are issued by the Foreign Agricultural Service. Some are regular weekly publications and others are released at specified dates during the year. They contain data on individual agricultural commodities and on regional and world developments in commodities, programs, and policies.

The Foreign Agricultural Service considers that personnel interested in becoming agricultural attaches require a background in agricultural economics and agricultural marketing. Normally, the successful applicant is a graduate of an agricultural college. Although it is preferred that the candidate have a knowledge of the language and area before assuming an assignment overseas, this is not always possible. The ability to read, write, and speak a foreign language is considered valuable, but not essential.

Description and Problems. The Foreign Agricultural Service hires agricultural college graduates—most of whom eventually become members of the overseas Agricultural Attache Service—at GS-5 [2] or GS-7 levels from among those who take the Federal Service entrance examination and successfully qualify under the agricultural economics option. A few may come in at the GS-9 level by unassembled examination, that is, by a test based on experience and references, not a formal, written examination. The Foreign Agricultural Service is now adding about twelve to fifteen young employees at the professional level each year. It has indicated that professional competence at this level has improved since the Agricultural Attache Service was separated from the Foreign Service. At present, 125 professional employees of the Foreign Agricultural Service have served or are serving overseas as members of the Agricultural Attache Service. Two-thirds are in the field and the rest are in the Department. Candidates for the Agricultural Attache Service are not selected for overseas service until they have completed three or more years with the Foreign Agricultural Service in the United States on assignments in at least two different areas of activity. During service in the Department, potential candidates for the attache service are encouraged to take language or other courses in the Foreign Service Institute or in the Department of Agriculture's Graduate School. By the time they are selected as junior assistants for one of the sixty-one overseas posts which serve American agricultural interests in 100 countries, employees have usually achieved a GS-11 rating. In the past, a few were sent overseas as GS-9s with little experience, but this is now viewed as a mistake.

No one older than fifty-five is sent from the Foreign Agricultural Service to serve for the first time as an agricultural attache unless he has had previous overseas experience with another government agency or in a private capacity. No one is returned overseas to start

---

[2] The normal General Schedule grade assigned to a college graduate entering the Civil Service is GS-5. GS-15 was for a time the top-ranking grade in the Civil Service. In recent years, promotions have been available within the Civil Service to three so-called supergrades: GS-16, GS-17, and GS-18.

another tour after the age of sixty-five, unless an exception is made by the Secretary of Agriculture.

A Personnel Assignment Committee, composed of assistant administrators of the Foreign Agricultural Service, considers appointments and watches careers. The attache service has administrative arrangements to provide flexibility in overseas assignments, but does have problems of interchangeability between the field and Washington staffs because of the small size of the Foreign Agricultural Service and the grade schedule of positions in the headquarters office. The attache service is allowed three GS-17 and nine GS-16 ratings. At ten overseas posts, the highest position is GS-15 to GS-17. At five posts, the top is GS-14 to GS-16. Most posts are headed by men with GS-13 or GS-14 ratings.

There is no "rank-in-man" concept—appointment to a class rather than to a specific post—in the Civil Service system, under which the attache service functions, but, as is true in the Foreign Service and the military services, various other devices are employed to insure that members of the attache service are not penalized by assignment to jobs with low ratings when they return to the Department after overseas tours. In a few instances, this has meant that high-ranking officers returning from overseas are assigned to administrative positions broader than their original specialties or attache responsibilities.

The performances of attache service personnel are evaluated not only on the basis of the Civil Service evaluation system but also on a system quite similar to that of the Foreign Service. It is believed by Foreign Agricultural Service officials that an agricultural attache can stay in the field most of the time for ten to twenty years without retraining with no serious impairment of his ability as an agricultural specialist.

The Foreign Agricultural Service has had little difficulty in finding enough young GS-11s or GS-12s who are interested in attache service. Its major problem is to find GS-13s and GS-14s moving successfully up the career ladder in Washington who are willing to take overseas posts. Men at this level do not want to interrupt their domestic careers, and they are also very particular about where they will go. Since they are in the Civil Service, they are not required to accept overseas assignment, whether it is of immediate interest to them or not.

Overseas duty is normally for a two-year period followed by home leave. Persons are not assigned to hardship posts for more than two years unless they ask to be reassigned. The typical pattern for overseas service is said to be three tours of two years each, followed by rotation to Washington for a two-year assignment. They usually go into the Foreign Agricultural Service when they are on Washington assignments even though they were not originally selected from it.

The Foreign Agricultural Service believes that its own personnel are more valuable after they return from overseas assignment than were Foreign Service officers assigned to work in the Department of Agriculture during the period when overseas agricultural marketing and reporting responsibilities were under the Foreign Service. Many of the Agricultural Attache Service personnel are said to value the Department of Agriculture as a home base from which to operate. Recently, on the occasion of the Department's hundredth anniversary, a conference of attaches was held in Washington, partly to strengthen this sense of identification with the Department of Agriculture. The Department believes that its best officers are no longer drained off as they once were by the Foreign Service to work in broader economic positions, leaving lower quality personnel to perform agricultural attache tasks. Furthermore, the Department believes that it has raised the professional level of its overseas representation following re-establishment of its separate service in 1954. The top salary for GS-17s is $17,500. On the other hand, it may be noted that a Class 1 Foreign Service officer or Reserve officer may receive up to $19,600.[3] Agriculture admits that this disparity constitutes a continual problem.

In certain aspects of mid-career or senior-level in-service training for overseas responsibilities the Department of Agriculture probably participates very little. Only two of its officers have enrolled in the mid-career course at the Foreign Service Institute. Three others have attended or are attending the senior seminar at the Institute. Lack of in-service training at mid-career and senior levels is attributed to the difficulty of keeping all the jobs filled.

Personnel in the agricultural field have also shown only limited interest in foreign languages. Agriculture officials recognize that the language barrier has been a serious deterrent to many in the Department who might otherwise be interested in overseas assignments.

There appears to be very little liaison in Washington at the present time between personnel of the Foreign Agricultural Service and the Foreign Service. The Department of Agriculture is represented on the Board of the Foreign Service and takes part in meetings. Its representatives play a less active role than formerly, since the Department is no longer associated closely with the Foreign Service. There is a brief exchange of ideas between the Department and the Foreign Service Inspection Corps once a year for about an hour and a half. The Corps does not formally inspect the work of the agricultural

---

[3] The Foreign Service classes begin with Class 8 and go up through Class 1. Above Class 1 are the Career Minister and Career Ambassador.

attaches but does talk with them in the course of its regular inspections at embassies and consulates. Agricultural personnel assigned overseas are cleared with the Department of State in Washington and with the ambassador and by the foreign government concerned before being sent. They are subject to removal from their posts by the ambassador for misconduct or for other reasons. Although the Foreign Agricultural Service expects its agricultural attaches to work closely with the economic section of the embassy and although they are normally given office space adjacent to it, the agricultural attaches report directly to the Department of Agriculture, sending copies to the Department of State. Attaches must clear matters pertaining to United States foreign policy with the ambassador.

Future Requirements. Some expansion in the number of posts and attaches is going on. At the time of writing, there were 64 foreign capitals with agricultural attaches and two one-man market centers [4] in Milan and Hamburg. The total projected staff in the Foreign Agricultural Service was 856 in 1964; 956 in 1965; 1,044 in 1966, and 1,132 in 1967, or an ultimate increase over the 1962 strength of about 65 per cent. It has been admitted, however, that this was optimistic and the actual growth rate is likely to be lower. So far as the attache service is concerned, the increase will undoubtedly be in assistant attaches rather than in any major expansion of posts or senior attaches. Per capita costs are likely to go up in spite of the greater use of junior-level personnel because of a steady but gradual rise in salaries of foreign personnel and in the cost of administrative support and rents.

No major changes are envisioned for personnel qualifications in the future. The Agricultural Attache Service will still need personnel with backgrounds in agricultural economics or agricultural marketing and several years of experience in the Department of Agriculture. Foreign Agricultural Service leaders hope that more programs in international affairs will be offered in agricultural institutions of higher learning so that recruits with language and area knowledge will be available.

Department of the Treasury: The Office of International Affairs (Treasury Representatives)

Functions. Treasury representatives are financial specialists who observe and report on financial and monetary developments relating to a country's balance-of-payments, reserve, and exchange rate situation.

---

[4] A market center is a small branch post established to operate in an important business center other than a national capital.

Their reports are made through normal State Department channels and are used, *inter alia,* in connection with operations of the Federal Reserve System and the Department of the Treasury in foreign exchange markets. They must have the ability to negotiate effectively with the financial officials of foreign governments. Most are specialized economic reporters, concentrating on financial conditions. They serve as senior members of the embassy's economic teams.

The role of the Treasury representatives is particularly important in view of the Department of the Treasury's role of policy adviser to the President on the fiscal implications of United States policies in foreign countries. Forecasts by the Treasury representatives on balance-of-payments developments in Western Europe and elsewhere are an essential element in forecasts of the probable course of the United States balance of payments.

Development and Size. After a decade of ad hoc representation overseas at intervals and for special purposes, the first Treasury representative of a more permanent nature was assigned to London in 1939 by the Secretary of the Treasury. Since that time, the number of Treasury representatives overseas has increased to sixteen and the number of posts abroad to ten, including posts in Western Europe, Southern Asia, the Far East, and Latin America. Posts have either a single man or a senior representative assisted by a junior representative. A single representative of the Treasury's Foreign Assets Control department is stationed in Hong Kong. The representatives are assisted by American clerical personnel, plus a local employee in a few instances. Staff for the overseas offices is drawn from the regular professional and clerical personnel of the Washington office. Total personnel strength of the Treasury Department's Office of International Affairs is approximately 150, of which about a third are economists and the balance supporting personnel.

Description and Problems. Potential Treasury representatives are normally recruited at the beginning of their careers as employees of the Office of International Affairs. In the past, the roster of individuals who had passed the Federal Service entrance examination and the management intern examination was carefully screened for young economists, preferably those with master's degrees who had specialized in fiscal or financial economics and had an interest in international affairs. They entered the Civil Service as GS-9s. Since these recruits were Civil Service personnel with no obligation for overseas service, they were not screened for foreign language ability, although such an ability was a factor in their favor. Good applicants have become harder to find in recent years; the Treasury Department attributes this to the fact that many of the best young people are being drawn into the study of the physical sciences today rather than into the study of the social sciences, as was the case in the 1930s.

Recruits are assigned to positions in the Office of International Affairs and work under the direction of senior officers. They are given on-the-job training, but also participate in orientation sessions sponsored by The Brookings Institution, the Civil Service Commission, or by the Department of the Treasury itself. Although there are no formal mid-career training programs, the Treasury Department has assigned individuals of intermediate and senior grade for participation in the program of the National War College and in the senior seminar of the Foreign Service Institute.

Junior economists selected for overseas assignment are sent, after a year or more of service in Washington, to a two-man post where they serve as Assistant Treasury representatives under the supervision of a more experienced man. The duration of assignments overseas varies, depending upon the interests of the man assigned. A Treasury representative may serve many years in a single country. Rotation of more experienced representatives is ordinarily done only at the request of the individual, but less experienced younger men are rotated as a training device.

Individuals are free to return to positions in the Office of International Affairs at the end of a tour if they no longer wish overseas assignments. There is no system of selection-out.[5] Personnel are brought into the Office of International Affairs after overseas duty at the same General Schedule level in which they had been serving abroad. There is some loss of able Treasury personnel because of the small number of assignments available in the Department at levels above GS-15. Assignments overseas at large posts are at senior levels, but small posts may be filled by individuals of intermediate grade. Treasury representatives cannot be appointed to top embassy positions, such as economic counselor or economic minister, without accepting a Foreign Service Reserve appointment. They may, however, have an unofficial title of minister in certain special situations. The Department has been unwilling to transfer such personnel to the Foreign Service Reserve and to reimburse the Department of State for their salaries and allowances.

The relationship of Treasury representatives to their embassies generally has been considered very good by officials of both the Treasury and State Departments. Treasury representatives usually

---

[5] The term selection-out refers to the removal of a Foreign Service officer who, within a given period of time, has not been promoted from one Class to the next or who, within a shorter time period, has not maintained a satisfactory level of performance. The maximum period an officer can stay in a given Class is established by the Secretary of State.

enjoy a status in the embassy commensurate with their experience and special contribution to the economic team. They use the State Department's communications channels, and their offices are in embassy buildings. The Department of State is reimbursed by the Department of the Treasury for these administrative services. Treasury representatives overseas are paid directly by the Department of the Treasury.

In Washington the relationship between the two departments has included the placement of two of the Treasury Department's top economists in the State Department and acceptance of two of State's economists in Treasury on a one-year exchange basis. Junior staff members in the Treasury Department gain an understanding of foreign policy interests by "back seat" attendance at interagency conferences involving the foreign affairs agencies and the Department of the Treasury.

Future Requirements. Personnel needs have been projected several years into the future. The Treasury Department anticipates a need for representation in a number of the less developed countries and hopes to add five more overseas representatives by 1965.

Atomic Energy Commission: Division of International Affairs (AEC Scientific Representatives)

Functions. Atomic Energy Commission scientific representatives are sent abroad primarily to assist in the implementation of the Atomic Energy Act of 1954, which provided that the United States could seek agreements with foreign countries to exchange nuclear information and to export certain nuclear materials and reactors. Such agreements are normally negotiated in Washington under the aegis of the Department of State with the AEC participating and handling the technical aspects of the negotiations, while overseas representatives both maintain the continuing relationships with the atomic energy establishments of foreign countries necessary for carrying out the agreements and report on the technical aspects of atomic energy developments abroad. They may assist the ambassador on diplomatic or other reporting functions related to atomic energy, but in practice limit themselves largely to technical reporting. Assigned on a regional basis, the scientific representatives investigate possible projects for cooperative effort between the United States and a foreign country or assist in the conduct of already established joint ventures.

Development, Size, and Qualifications. In the past, before development of major domestic sources of raw materials for the production

21

of atomic energy, the AEC's Raw Materials Division had extensive representation overseas. Its personnel checked on supplies of raw materials and were not tied closely to the United States embassies overseas. Today, only two such positions are staffed abroad, one in Canada and the other in Africa. Overseas representation of the AEC is now primarily the responsibility of the Commission's Division of International Affairs.

The Atomic Energy Act of 1954, which followed President Dwight D. Eisenhower's speech at the United Nations on the peaceful uses of atomic energy in 1953, expanded cooperative efforts in the field. By 1956 arrangements had been completed with the Department of State for AEC scientific representatives to serve abroad. During World War II, an office was established in Chalk River, Canada, by the Manhattan District; it has been maintained up to the present time. In 1956 and 1957, liaison offices were established in London, Paris, Tokyo, and Buenos Aires. In 1958 an office was opened in Brussels, primarily to maintain relations with the European Atomic Energy Community and the European Economic Community. In general, the offices consist of the scientific representative (sometimes with a professional-level assistant) and secretarial support. The Brussels office is headed by a senior AEC representative and includes four other professional-level employees.

Fourteen professional-level employees and nine secretaries are now serving full time overseas. The AEC is exempt from the mandatory requirements of the Classification Act,[6] but is subject to a merit system which ensures that each job will be filled on a merit basis by selecting the available individual best qualified in terms of the carefully determined requirements of the particular position and in accordance with the Veterans Preference Act of 1944 as amended.

Major qualifications required of personnel for professional posts are technical atomic knowledge and administrative competence. Experience with the AEC either in Washington or in one of its field offices is considered valuable. Assignments overseas (other than secretarial) are made at GS-12 to GS-17 levels or in the Scientific and Technical Schedule at pay levels up to $20,000 per year. Overseas posts usually include more technical responsibilities than do many of the administrative technical posts in the United States from which the scientific representatives are often selected.

Description and Problems. When the Division of International Affairs learns that it will have a professional-level post overseas to

---

[6] The Classification Act of 1949, as amended, provides for the classification of positions in federal agencies on the basis of duties and responsibilities, and for the fixing of salaries in accordance with this classification.

fill, it notifies the Division of Personnel. This division then makes up a list of about 100 possible candidates drawn from throughout the AEC. An informal screening by the Divisions of International Affairs and Personnel cuts the number of candidates by half. Then a three-man committee, with several divisions represented and with a representative of the Division of Personnel serving as secretary, further reduces the list to between three and ten candidates who are certified as qualified. These individuals are interviewed and finally selected by the Director of the Division of International Affairs.

Overseas appointments are normally for one two-year period with the possibility of a one-year extension. Technical personnel sometimes find it difficult to accept overseas duty because of family problems, but the assignment is generally viewed as a pleasant one, since no posts are located in hardship areas. There has been no problem of finding domestic appointments at a similar level for men returning from tours abroad. The small number of AEC employees abroad often receive the attention of their superiors as a result of their service and are in demand upon their return.

The AEC now follows the practice of initiating recruitment of a replacement eight months prior to the end of the tour of an overseas employee. One purpose of this is to ensure adequate time for orderly orientation. It also provides for an overlap at the post.

Technical personnel for overseas offices are now almost always selected from within the Commission. Because of their familiarity with the program they can ordinarily obtain adequate technical orientation in two or three weeks of interviews in Washington and at some of the major technical facilities. Appropriate briefings at the Department of State on political, economic, and social developments in the territory of assignment are arranged by the State Department's Office of International Scientific Affairs.

Once a candidate has been selected for overseas assignment, he is informed of courses at the Foreign Service Institute which he may take prior to his departure. An effort is also made for the candidate, and in some cases members of his family, to attend briefing courses. Usually the appointee's schedule is so tight that Foreign Service Institute language courses cannot be utilized, and therefore individual arrangements are made for this training both before and after arrival at his post.

The AEC's present inclination is not to view overseas service as a special career. If appointments were made for more than three years, technical personnel would have to be returned to the United States for extensive reorientation in the Commission's program. Technical material from the Commission's library is available to personnel on overseas assignment upon request. Many of the persons assigned here have been drawn from technical positions with administrative requirements. The overseas assignments are considered an opportunity to advance their technical knowledge during the period.

Few of the Commission's potential candidates for overseas duty would be interested in overseas service on a career basis, since they are on their way up in a technical specialty for which overseas service is a step and not a final goal. The opportunity for a wide number of AEC employees to be considered for appointment to overseas duty is believed to have helped recruiting for jobs with the Commission.

The head of the Buenos Aires office has had diplomatic status since the office was opened; it has recently been accorded the head of the London office. The possibility of extending diplomatic status to additional AEC overseas employees is now under study in the Department of State. AEC offices are normally in embassy buildings, and the representatives are attached to the political or economic sections.

Future Requirements. Personnel requirements overseas in the atomic energy field are considered to be stable. Some preliminary consideration has been given by the AEC to the possibility of establishing a liaison office in Southern Asia. No significant changes in the number of personnel at individual posts are foreseen.

In the past there was a tendency for the senior official at each post to be a technical specialist and the junior person primarily an administrator. Although the AEC has no intention of assigning personnel to second terms overseas at a later point in their careers, consideration will be given to a promising former junior representative if he is later interested in a second appointment abroad.

RELATED PROGRAMS
Department of Commerce (Commercial Specialist Program)

In the Department of Commerce, the writer centered his attention on the new relationship of the commercial specialization to the Foreign Service of the United States, as defined by the Memorandum of Agreement between the Department of State and the Department of Commerce of November 15, 1961.[7] By 1961 the number of commercial specialists in the Foreign Service had increased to only 129 from 105 in 1939. Pressure for expansion of the commercial specialization began mounting in the late 1950s when United States

---

[7] See Appendix B.

24

balance-of-payments difficulties became serious. The Senate Committee on Interstate and Foreign Commerce devoted considerable attention to these problems in hearings which occurred early in 1960. There followed in 1961 the passage of the Engle Bill in the Senate which included a section to create a separate Foreign Commerce Service. This proposal did not reach the floor of the House of Representatives.

A reorganization within the Department of Commerce at the end of October 1962 centered the Department's domestic and international business activities related to national security interests of the United States under an Assistant Secretary for Domestic and International Business. The new Assistant Secretary was to be responsible for the Business and Defense Services Administration and the Bureau of International Commerce, as well as an Office of Field Services to serve domestic field offices of the Department of Commerce, an Office of Trade Adjustment, and an Office of Foreign Commercial Services. This last office was to serve as the bridge between the Department of Commerce and the Department of State to coordinate the commercial specialization established by the State-Commerce Agreement with the Foreign Service.

Functions of Commercial Attaches and Commercial Officers. Commercial specialists report on the commercial activities of foreign countries as an aspect of the economic reporting of embassies and as an aid to United States business. They may also be assigned to do economic reporting covering a broader field than their commercial specialty. Commercial specialists develop a knowledge of the needs of foreign importers and of the resources for export that are of interest to American businessmen and manufacturers. They assist visiting United States Trade Missions. They have been asked to stimulate private United States investment in less developed countries and private investment from more industrialized countries in the United States.

In addition, the commercial specialists advise the ambassador on matters of commercial policy, and provide commercial information when needed to other members of the country team. Through their assistance in suggesting exhibits that would be useful at trade centers, they play an important role in creating the image of the United States abroad.

In a specific listing of the duties of commercial attaches and officers, the Department of Commerce indicates commercial specialists perform some 24 reporting functions, 34 commercial services, 26 trade promotion operations, and 17 market research and development activities. In addition, they are expected to perform 25 administrative functions in the organization and direction of their substantive tasks. Emphasis at the present time is on the active development of markets to promote trade expansion, but commercial reporting for both business and policy purposes remains important.

At the discretion of posts overseas, commercial specialists may be assigned to investigate foreign importers in order to prevent the trans-shipment of American goods to communist countries. The Department of Commerce is primarily responsible for the administration of export controls. The reporting that is necessary in this connection is normally the responsibility of economic officers overseas. Commercial officers do assist in this work at certain posts, however.

Development, Size, and Qualifications. United States interest in business and trade opportunities overseas is not new. Commercial agents were stationed abroad to serve the government in the late eighteenth century. Commercial reporting and trade promotion were among the important functions of the Consular Service before the Diplomatic and Consular Services were joined by the Rogers Act of 1924 to become the Foreign Service of the United States. Since that time, except for a twelve-year period from 1927 to 1939 when a corps of commercial attaches and trade commissioners was operated separately by the Department of Commerce, the commercial attache function has been performed by officers of the Foreign Service. As trade controls became more important than trade expansion in the period before World War II, the 105 officers of the separate Commerce services were integrated into the Foreign Service. Presently there are 149 commercial specialists authorized in the Foreign Service, with an additional forty-eight requested for 1964. Of the present number, more than 100 are regular Foreign Service officers and forty are Foreign Service Reserve officers. Half of the latter group are Department of Commerce officers on temporary duty abroad. The other half, practically all of whom have had considerable business experience, are recruits from outside the government.

The United States is now entering a period of strong emphasis on trade promotion as the result of balance-of-payments difficulties since 1959. By legislation, the Department of Commerce has for some time been responsible for the promotion abroad of trade, travel, and investment. The President reiterated this fact in 1961 when he specifically vested primary responsibility for trade expansion in the Department of Commerce. This directive, coupled with the Engle Bill to set up a Foreign Commerce Service necessitated giving the Department of Commerce a stronger role in the Foreign Service or allowing the Department of Commerce to recreate a separate service. Thus, the

State-Commerce Agreement of November 15, 1961, allowed the Department of Commerce a greater voice in the control of commercial specialists in the Foreign Service.

Commercial officers require a knowledge of economics and of more specialized subject matter related to commercial and business activities. Usually they have been drawn from among liberal arts college graduates who have majored in economics or from schools of business. However, some business experience and a period of service in the Department of Commerce are now considered desirable. With rather diverse functions to be performed, it may be anticipated that there will be a further degree of specialization within the commercial specialization. It seems likely that an additional number of employees of the Department of Commerce and some personnel from business will be appointed as Foreign Service Reserve officers within the next several years to stimulate trade promotion activities.

The Department of State hopes to preserve a ratio of at least two Foreign Service officers to one Foreign Service Reserve officer in the commercial specialization. Career officers now occupy more than 70 per cent of the Commercial Specialist Program positions abroad, and over 80 per cent of the total inclusive of Washington rotational assignments. Since 1956, there has been an agreement between the State and Commerce Departments whereby an exchange program provides for foreign assignments of twenty domestic Commerce officers against a similar number of Foreign Service officers rotated in substantive Washington assignments to the Department of Commerce.

Description and Problems. It is difficult to assess properly the tenor of the relationship between the Department of Commerce and the Foreign Service of the United States in the period since 1939. There are those who believe that the Commerce Department has always been rather belligerent in insisting upon better reporting to meet its needs and upon the opportunity to train Foreign Service officers to do more adequate commercial work overseas. The Department is a member of the Board of the Foreign Service and has had representation on most if not all of the Board's subsidiary bodies. Yet, others claim that the Department found itself at a disadvantage and unable to participate as an equal, and that the State Department maintained an undue measure of control in such matters as staffing complements for the commercial function and assignments and generally did not play as positive and responsive a role as it might have in meeting the specialized needs of the program. On the other hand, it should be noted that the Department of State functions under a tight budget and finds it difficult to obtain sufficient appropriations to meet its own needs as well as those of Commerce and other departments served by the Foreign Service. The State Department does realize it is imperative to assign a higher priority to the tasks performed for other departments. Any present lack of responsiveness by the State Department is more likely to stem from continued fund shortages than from a failure to comprehend growing needs.

Recruitment of potential commercial officers for the integrated Foreign Service at the FSO-8 level was conducted previously by recruiters sent to college campuses from the Foreign Service or the Department of State without Department of Commerce participation. Recruiters found the most interest in Foreign Service careers among students with political science, history, economics, or international affairs training. It has been suggested, however, that recruiters seldom had the opportunity, and did not seek it until recently, to talk with students interested in business careers or in commercial activities. Under the new agreement, Department of Commerce employees and Foreign Service officers with a commercial specialization are expected to participate and to encourage students attending the better schools of business to pursue Foreign Service careers.

Although the entrance examinations for the Foreign Service have varied in content through the years, students with training in business and commercial affairs have rarely found their training an advantage in taking the examination. As a matter of fact, the subject matter of the examination usually placed these students at some disadvantage. The addition of an optional commercial and administrative section on the Foreign Service examination in 1963 was intended to encourage students from schools of business to display their abilities and make their selection more likely—in the same way as adequate representation of the Department of Commerce or of commercial officers on oral examination panels.

In the past, young Foreign Service officers rarely sought commercial specialization, nor did they seek assignments in the Department of Commerce as part of their early training; their interests were oriented toward political or general economic work. Because of the nature of traditional United States foreign policy, with its political or economic concern and reporting emphasis, commercial work was not greatly emphasized or valued within the Foreign Service. Although they were exposed to some orientation in the commercial field, most young Foreign Service officers were afraid that if they displayed too much interest or talent in this field they would be tabbed as commercial specialists. Changing conditions and new needs have increased the importance of the commercial specialization. Young officers who take the commercial option on the examination are more likely to

28

seek assignment to the Department of Commerce as part of their early training and to take full advantage of commercial orientation offered at the Foreign Service Institute.

It is anticipated by those implementing the State-Commerce Agreement that young officers will not normally opt officially for the commercial specialization until they are about ready to enter FSO-6. It is possible that the twig can be well bent by that time so that a sufficient number of those exposed to commercial work will actually elect it as a career. Furthermore, commercial specialists will need to worry less about giving up their specialization at FSO-3 or FSO-2 in order to achieve further promotion, if promotions in this and in other fields of specialization are made possible to the rank of FSO-1. Moreover, three positions of counselor rank have already been allocated to the commercial field. A further increase in the number of commercial counselors is still under discussion in the State Department. An alternative procedure has been the designation of a single economic and commercial counselor with additional appointments in this category also contemplated.

There is some fear within the Department of Commerce that recognition of a commercial specialization may make it more difficult for personnel in this field to participate in the over-all economic work of the embassy, but it is generally understood that at points during their careers commercial specialists will be assigned to economic positions for the purpose of broadening their background. This would imply a continued recognition of the close relationship of commercial work to economic reporting and policy advisory functions.

A major element of the State-Commerce Agreement was the shifting of budget responsibilities for the commercial specialization from the Department of State to the Department of Commerce. This provision was opposed by the Bureau of the Budget, which thought such an arrangement would so blur lines of responsibility and authority as to make ineffective the operation of the Commercial Specialist Program that was set up under the Agreement.[8]

For the year 1963,[9] the Department of Commerce was allowed to ask Congress for additional positions in the commercial specialization, but the Department of State retained responsibility for obtaining appropriations for the existing commercial officer positions. Congress objected to having funds for the same purpose requested by two agencies and turned down the Department of Commerce request. In 1964,

---

[8] This is the formal title used for the commercial specialization policy established in the State-Commerce Agreement. See Appendix B, Part IV.

[9] In this case and in subsequent references to a particular year, the author is referring to the fiscal year.

the Department of State is to be responsible for the total budget needs for the commercial specialization in foreign affairs.

An important section of the State-Commerce Agreement calls for the establishment of a separate commercial school in the Foreign Service Institute. The head is to be designated by the Secretary of Commerce with the concurrence of the Secretary of State. The Commerce Department is also to assume greater responsibility for communications to and from commercial specialists in the field. The increased participation of the Department of Commerce is the result of the recognition that it should have primary responsibility for promoting foreign trade while the State Department continues to have primary responsibility for foreign economic policy. This division, combined with a stronger position for the Department of Commerce, has brought some question as to whom the commercial officers should really be responsible under the terms of the original agreement. To a certain extent, this accounts for the Bureau of the Budget's criticism of the State-Commerce Agreement that places commercial specialists as formal members of the Foreign Service while financial support is part of the Commerce Department's budget.

In a recommendation of December 5, 1961, intended as an alternative to the State-Commerce Agreement, the Bureau of the Budget advocated removing the trade promotion program and closely allied activities from the commercial specialization within the Foreign Service. The purpose of this proposal was to separate trade promotion from representation, policy interpretation, and negotiation. For the reason that such a line could not be fruitfully drawn between the various elements of commercial work overseas, neither State nor Commerce has publicly supported this position to date; both agencies have officially supported the present agreement. A fair analysis of this issue would indicate that the trade promotion responsibility could probably be met either by following the Bureau of the Budget recommendation or by working within the State-Commerce Agreement. On balance, unless the trade promotion program is viewed as a large-scale temporary operation, the advantages of close cooperation within the Foreign Service outweigh those of a separate service. If trade promotion continues to be important in the foreseeable future, the State-Commerce Agreement seems flexible enough to meet program needs.

Future Requirements. Some Department of Commerce officials look forward to the rapid expansion of the commercial specialization from the present 149 officers to almost 400 specialists. This goal seems unlikely of realization. As personnel interviewed in Commerce admitted, it is not difficult to project needs, but it is difficult to obtain the funds and personnel to fill them. Officially, the Department hopes to expand the Commercial Specialist Program abroad to about 200 officers in 1964, with perhaps a further increase of 25 per cent in 1965. The Department's highest estimate, which includes personnel for trade fairs, trade centers, and other related activities, has been a limit of 300 officers.

There is a desire on the part of some Department of Commerce personnel to incorporate 50 to 100 of its employees in the commercial specialization of the Foreign Service as Foreign Service Reserve officers. However, it is not anticipated that the number going into the Foreign Service Reserve will exceed 25 to 30 in the next two years. There will be a drive to recruit personnel from private business into the Commercial Specialist Program, particularly if personnel for trade promotion and related activities remain within the Foreign Service. These increases also would apparently be made through appointments in the Foreign Service Reserve. Between 400 and 500 economic officers in the Foreign Service are presently said to be doing part-time commercial reporting, and it appears likely that they will continue.

Success in the new Trade Centers Program, less than two years old, could bring some increases in commercial positions overseas. Centers are now operating in Bangkok, London, Tokyo, Frankfurt, and Milan. The number will rise to twelve by 1965 if Congressional approval of an expansion of the program is forthcoming. The Trade Centers Program involves setting up exhibition halls and meeting rooms in which six to eight shows are held each year. The American products exhibited are those which market research indicates could be sold if foreign distributors and agents were obtained. The program tries to interest American firms in entering the overseas market by helping them find sales agents abroad. At present, each Trade Center is staffed by three full-time officers of the Commercial Specialist Program and five local employees. An exhibition officer from the Civil Service staff of the Department of Commerce is added briefly to handle housekeeping details for each show and is assisted by about seven local employees.

Supplementing the USIA Trade Fair Program, which has operated since 1954 primarily to project an image of the United States for psychological-political purposes, is a new Department of Commerce Trade Fair Program, which emphasizes trade expansion. Under this program a Civil Service exhibition officer is sent from the Department of Commerce into the field for a short working visit in connection with each of the seventeen annual USIA Trade Fair projects to help regular embassy employees take advantage of this program's possibilities for stimulating exports. Funds for participation by the Department of Commerce in seven trade fairs, primarily for expansion of trade were provided in 1963. The Commerce Department took part for the first time under the new program in a fair held at Utrecht on March 11, 1963, and by June in two more, at Lyons and Barcelona, and in four others during the autumn of 1963. The Department of Commerce has requested funds for participation in twelve fairs during 1964. American participation is supported by the regular embassy staff and by one temporary Civil Service exhibition officer sent overseas by the Commerce Department who services visitors during the fair and works under the general direction of the commercial attache.

Since 1954, the Department of Commerce has supported a number of exploratory trips overseas by trade missions, composed of American businessmen seeking sales abroad. The Department of Commerce now staffs thirteen such missions annually. Each trade mission requires one Civil Service officer who may spend two or three months working on a particular mission in advance of its going overseas. In addition, each mission may require two or three Civil Service officers as leaders who remain overseas for periods of approximately a month with the members of the mission. Some preparatory work is required by the regular economic and commercial staff in the embassy in preparation for the visit by a trade mission. A program for miniature displays of samples of American products in more out-of-the-way places than those where trade centers will be established or trade fairs held sometimes requires another small increment in personnel. A limited number of personnel will also be required to staff the expanding travel service of the Department of Commerce, but these are Civil Service rather than Foreign Service officers. Continued support of this program in the embassies and consulates, however, could result in a slight increase in the number of commercial specialists required in the Foreign Service.

If Congress were to insist on more overseas investigations of applications from foreign importers for permission to import American goods, and should the need for export controls continue, there could be a further increase in commercial positions. Very little expansion of the economic officer complement has been envisioned by the State Department.

There are natural limits to what the government can do to stimulate trade in a private enterprise economy. Commercial specialists in the Foreign Service or in a separate overseas service can supply information, assist businessmen in making contacts with foreign business interests, and suggest general guidelines. They cannot do the total sales job themselves. Furthermore, many factors other than sales bear heavily on the results that can be expected: for example, cost factors, or the economic and political stability of foreign governments. Thus, the need for an expansion of commercial specialists in or outside the Foreign Service has natural limits. However, there may be a growing need for "sub-specialists" within the commercial field both in and outside the Commercial Specialist Program of the Foreign Service.

Department of Labor (Labor Attaches)

For this study, attention was focused on the relationship of the Department of Labor to the staffing of the labor attache program which is supposed to be completely integrated within the Foreign Service of the United States. Department of Labor participation is the responsibility of the Bureau of International Labor Affairs.

Functions of Labor Attaches. Labor attaches develop and maintain close contacts with foreign trade union leaders, with government labor officials, and with foreign management officials for the purpose of gathering and appraising information on foreign labor movements and developments. They report on the economic and political aspects of labor events and try to promote an understanding of the United States and its foreign policies in labor circles. They also serve as advisers on labor matters to the ambassador and other members of the embassy.

Labor attaches are eager to offer guidance on labor projects in technical assistance and cultural exchange programs. They sometimes participate as members of United States delegations in international conferences dealing with matters that may affect labor in the country to which they are appointed. By establishing contacts with local labor leaders they can often help visiting trade union delegations to obtain information.

In the past, labor attaches served primarily as technical support for the policy needs of the Department of State. Today, however, labor attaches also give assistance to American labor organizing unions abroad. Foreign labor organizations are often aligned with political parties and have become an increasingly important political and economic power factor. The assistance given by labor attaches to American labor organizing abroad not only contributes to the achievement of the Department of State's foreign policy goals but also may benefit American labor unions. Recently, labor attaches have been active in furthering the study of labor factor costs in the production of foreign commodities; they have sometimes taken action overseas that is helpful to Department of Labor programs in the United States.

Development and Size. The first labor representative was sent to

London unofficially in 1939, but the labor attache program was actually initiated by the Foreign Service of the United States in 1943 when attaches were sent to Buenos Aires and Santiago. The program was expanded to eight officers by 1944 and to fifteen by 1945. Prior to 1946 appointments were made by the Department of State after only informal consultation with the Department of Labor. Since the enactment of the Foreign Service Act of 1946, which made the Department of Labor a member of the Board of the Foreign Service, the Department of Labor has played a more active role. Figures indicating the growth pattern of the Labor attache program show that there were 18 attaches in 1946; 21 by 1948; 23 by 1949; 30 by 1950; 33 by 1951; 28 by 1954; 36 by 1956; 39 by 1958; 49 by 1960; and 56 by 1962. At present there are 66. The reduction in number in 1954 parallels the cutback that faced the Department of Agriculture during the first Eisenhower Administration but was not as severe as the cutback in agricultural attaches. Some of the loss was successfully overcome by the assignment of Foreign Service officers as labor reporting officers on a part-time basis. There are approximately 100 of these labor reporting officers in the Foreign Service.

The labor attache program is now an integral part of the Foreign Service and functions under the Foreign Service Act of 1946 with what is generally felt to be adequate participation in all levels in the administration of the Foreign Service. Some Labor officials do not consider that labor staffing is as strong as it should be and note that many of the best officers today were drawn to the program immediately after World War II to assume heavy responsibilities in Japan, Germany, and France.

The qualifications for labor attaches include: a practical understanding of the political scene with an interest in international affairs; experience in the labor movement or in teaching labor relations; experience in the government labor field; some basic training in economics; and knowledge of a foreign language and a geographical area. Few labor attaches have all these qualifications.

Description and Problems. Although the Foreign Service examination contains no labor option, and emphasis in Foreign Service career recruiting has not been on labor specialists, almost half of the labor attaches now serving are career Foreign Service officers who have moved into the labor specialization as one phase of their total Foreign Service career. On the other hand, major elements of the labor attache program have been staffed by mid-career appointments into the Foreign Service Reserve from the Department of Labor and the American labor movement.

34

Recommendations on appointments to the Foreign Service Reserve are made by the Department of Labor. Candidates for appointment are given an oral examination by a panel consisting of Foreign Service officers and representatives of the Department of Labor. Each panel member judges those abilities and attributes in which he is most interested. If a candidate successfully passes the oral examination, the Department of State processes security and medical clearances.

There are many who believe that most of those taken into the labor attache program should not start at the bottom of the career ladder. Moreover, career Foreign Service officers are considered to be better at reporting the political aspects of labor affairs overseas than the Foreign Service Reserve officers drawn from the labor field who place more emphasis upon the development of overseas labor movements. According to one Labor Department official, "It takes many years to develop junior Foreign Service officers into competent labor attaches." On the other hand, staffing of the labor attache program by Reserve officers drawn from the labor movement has also been subject to criticism. Orientation for Foreign Service Reserve officers before assignment overseas has often been sketchy. For instance, there have been new officers who were sent overseas within a week after their appointment. It is recognized by some officials in the Department of Labor that individuals coming to the program from the labor movement actually need a year of orientation before going overseas, but they seldom, if ever, get such training. Many are sent without adequate knowledge of a foreign language.

The Department of Labor had almost no relationship with the career counseling and development program of the Foreign Service until mid-1962. Few Labor Reserve officers had participated before that time in mid-career training courses at the Foreign Service Institute. There has been some lateral entry of Reserve officers in the labor attache program into the Foreign Service as career Foreign Service Officers. The Labor Department is represented on the lateral-entry examining panels, and since 1958 only two Labor Reserve officers of twelve who sought to enter the Foreign Service permanently have been refused admission.

In the opinion of the Department of Labor, there has been an insufficient number of Foreign Service officers with labor specializations assigned to the Department of Labor for Washington assignments when they return to the United States on rotation. It is hoped that some of these returning officers will also at a future time be given training assignments with American labor unions. At present there are five positions in the Department of State and three in the Department of Labor in Washington that are held for returning labor attaches. The Department of Labor would like three more in its Department.

After reaching the FSO-3 or FSO-2 level, officers with a labor specialization are normally required to give up their specialty and broaden their careers. Several have done this successfully and have later served at top posts in embassies and consulates. Department of Labor personnel are pleased that the close relationship of labor affairs to political and economic affairs in many countries overseas has brought about a greater interest among Foreign Service officers in the labor specialization. On the other hand, it is noted that such Foreign Service officers normally select the specialization as a means of escaping from the less interesting categories of Foreign Service work and in turn hope to use the labor experience as a vehicle for moving into economic or political affairs.

Communications with the field via the Department of State have worked reasonably well from the standpoint of the Department of Labor. Reports from labor reporting officers in the Current Economic Reporting Program (CERP)[10] are considered to be of variable quality, as only 25 to 40 per cent of these officers have had any training in labor reporting. Reliance on such reporting is considered a "pot luck" approach. Labor recognizes that it has not pressed as hard as it might to solve some of the problems which exist in reporting and communication. There are a few in the Department of Labor who believe that communications with labor attaches should be more direct. It is said that when a dispatch comes to a country desk in the State Department with unfavorable comments from an ambassador it predisposes the desk officer to unfavorable action because of the desk officer's position in the Foreign Service career ladder. Only a

---

[10] The Current Economic Reporting Program provides for specialized economic reporting by overseas posts on a variety of topics to meet the needs of many agencies of the United States government. Responsibility for the program in Washington is centered in the Foreign Reporting Staff of the Bureau of Economic Affairs in the Department of State. Overseas programs of interest to domestic affairs agencies that are staffed by Foreign Service or Foreign Service Reserve officers are largely dependent upon this system of reporting to obtain information on economic conditions abroad relevant to policy-making and operations in areas where no attaches in their specialty are stationed.

Instructions to the field concerning the Current Economic Reporting Program fall under four headings. Section A calls for the post to be responsive not only to regular and repetitive reporting requirements but also to meet the special needs of the participating agencies. Section B covers reporting of primarily statistical material on production, foreign trade, and balance of payments, and also covers short narrative reports on commodities and industries—these latter often of interest to the Bureau of Mines or to the Bureau of Commercial Fisheries of the Department of the Interior. Section C includes general economic reports, which are a political-economic assessment in some depth of the present economic situation in a particular country, with a forecast of developing situations in terms of United States interests. It also provides for an unclassified economic summary, with materials for publication by the Department of Commerce, and for a biweekly economic review, putting important economic developments of each period covered in some perspective. Section C also includes an analysis of the labor situation in some depth, and its relationship to political developments where appropriate; a science report; and a bloc area report. Section D provides for non-periodic voluntary reporting from the field as anything of importance occurs, with changing guidance as to what important topics should be particularly watched.

small number of persons in the Labor Department believe that labor reports should come to that Department for analysis before being forwarded to State for action. Others feel that there is not presently an effective means of keeping labor attaches abreast of American labor developments while they are in the field. Some would like the Department of Labor to establish its own regional representation to carry out this responsibility.

Future Requirements. The Department of Labor recommended an increase of twenty-nine labor attaches in 1963, but the increase was not granted. It is unlikely that such a large increment would ever be allowed in a single year. However, in the next ten years there may be a steady growth in the number of labor attaches from the present level to between 120 and 130. Labor officials feel the need for a labor attache at each overseas post, as well as for assistant attaches in some of the larger embassies.

Individuals outside the Department of Labor have questioned the usefulness of Foreign Service Reserve officers chosen from the American labor movement as labor attaches in underdeveloped countries, noting the different nature of the union function in these countries from that which the union now performs in the United States. Others have wanted more emphasis on recruiting personnel with economic training or with a background that would fit them to study the labor and manpower resources required for development of the economies of new nations.

Federal Aviation Agency: International Aviation Service (Civil Aviation Attaches)[11]

Functions. The International Aviation Service of the Federal Aviation Agency (FAA) has an interest in a civil aviation attache function that is normally performed by regular officers in the Foreign Service of the United States. Foreign Service officers assigned this function report on civil aviation developments abroad and maintain relations with aviation interests in foreign countries. They advise ambassadors on the political, economic, and commercial implications of these developments.

Development and Size. Several FAA employees have indicated that as of June 1962 the importance of the civil aviation attache function

---

[11] Not considered in this study are the limited research and development activities of the Agency overseas, which involve five Civil Service employees of the Agency in research on "hardware and electronic systems." Also excluded from this survey are 17 technical assistance personnel furnished by the Agency to the International Civil Aviation Organization and 151 Agency personnel working overseas on Agency for International Development programs. These are carried on the personnel rolls of the Federal Aviation Agency and paid by the FAA with funds received through a reimbursement agreement with AID.

had not yet been sufficiently recognized by the Foreign Service. In 1962, only five Foreign Service officers were assigned on a full-time basis to perform civil aviation reporting or advisory functions. Ten Foreign Service officers, designated as transportation and communications officers, did part-time civil aviation reporting. In response to FAA needs, the State Department provided two additional civil aviation attaches in 1963, and two more are being sought for 1964.

Description and Problems. The FAA has an arrangement with the Department of State whereby the latter provides reporting services on civil aviation matters abroad. Although agency officials receive some 1,000 dispatches a month on aviation matters, the information is not always adequate or relevant to FAA needs. Most of the personnel assigned to the reporting tasks, either full- or part-time, have had little or no experience in the aviation industry. Several individuals interviewed did not believe the personnel entirely understand the implications of what they see and hear or are necessarily sympathetic to aviation programs. Personnel assigned to civil aviation reporting look at it as a temporary interlude in their Foreign Service careers and, even if able, apparently hesitate to become tabbed as specialists.

The FAA has about 45,000 employees. Several FAA officials believe the Agency and the Civil Aeronautics Board could find individuals from among their own employees who could be appointed at FSR-3, FSR-2, or FSR-1 levels, and do a better job than is being done. Agency officials did propose in 1962 that such individuals be appointed for four-year tours after a period of retraining and being brought up to date on American civil aviation developments. Such a program was accepted by the Department of State, and in January 1963 an experienced FAA employee was assigned as a Foreign Service Reserve officer in Lima and an experienced Civil Aeronautics Board employee was assigned as a Foreign Service Reserve officer in Lagos. The FAA has expressed satisfaction with the initiation of this program. The Agency does not object if regular Foreign Service officers also continue to be assigned as civil aviation reporting officers, on a full- or part-time basis.

Future Requirements. At the present time, FAA officials feel a need for full-time civil aviation representation at about twenty overseas posts, with some of the posts bearing responsibility for an entire region. Although they do not believe that one man can adequately serve either the whole African or the entire Latin American region, they have accepted the fact that broad regional representation is all that can reasonably be expected for certain areas in the immediate future.

Department of the Interior: Bureau of Mines (Minerals Attaches)

Functions. Minerals attaches perform economic and technological reporting functions for foreign policy makers, essential mineral supply planners, and American businessmen. In addition, they may provide information to foreign countries and institutions on drafting mining laws and organizing mining operations. Minerals attaches are interested in discovering how new ideas have been applied to the processing of mineral resources. These specialized attaches supposedly have professional entrée into the confidence of foreign specialists and American engineers operating abroad, which produces a more abundant and reliable exchange of information than is normally obtainable by the Foreign Service "generalist" officer.

Size and Development. In 1935 the Bureau of Mines was authorized to send representatives to foreign countries and in the years following did send a few specialists abroad. In 1943, however, they were incorporated into the Foreign Service. There are at present eight minerals attaches and at least four petroleum attaches in the Foreign Service. Minerals and petroleum reporting also is done by Foreign Service officers, who are not specialists, but the Bureau of Mines has asserted that this type of service does not adequately meet its needs.

Description and Problems. The specialized minerals attaches are normally Foreign Service Reserve officers who have entered overseas service at mid-career. The youngest ever sent out was thirty-five years of age at time of appointment. Most have had a close relationship with the minerals industry in the United States, with at least two years of work in the Department of Interior learning about government interests in the minerals field. Minerals attaches have the right to return to the Department of Interior. They are not encouraged to join the Foreign Service and aim for the top positions. Men who have served as minerals attaches, in fact, often do return to the Bureau of Mines where they are quickly absorbed into the programs of the Bureau.

The Bureau of Mines has expressed the opinion that it is not allowed to participate sufficiently in evaluating the over-all performance of minerals attaches. It also believes that its views are not properly considered by promotion panels. The Current Economic Reporting Program has been cut recently, and the minerals section of the CERP report is now considered inadequate. The Bureau of Mines is dependent upon this system of reporting for information in countries where special minerals or petroleum attaches are not stationed. Furthermore, it is said, minerals attaches are "short-changed" on secretarial and travel funds.

Enforced retirement of career Foreign Service officers at the age of sixty presents a problem. In recent years, two outstanding minerals specialists were forced out of the Foreign Service at that age, thus— according to the Bureau of Mines—depriving the technical agencies and United States mining interests of the services of these highly competent engineers. Although the age limit does not apply to Reserve officers, it does interfere with the assignment of technical attaches. The State Department appears to discourage nominations of candidates who are approaching their sixtieth year even if they are exceptionally well qualified professionally and physically.

The Bureau of Mines has pointed out that it has pleaded for an adequate minerals attache staff in the Foreign Service for many years. According to Bureau of Mines officials, this objective has not been given a high enough priority by the Department of State.

Future Requirements. The outlook for expansion in the number of minerals attaches is somewhat bleak, according to the Bureau of Mines, mostly because the Department of State believes that nonspecialized officers in the Foreign Service can perform minerals reporting functions. The Bureau of Mines expressed a need for an additional twenty-two men, of whom five would be petroleum specialists. This program, the Bureau points out, was endorsed in the mineral resources chapter of a recent report on research needs in the natural resources field prepared under the auspices of the National Academy of Science at the request of the President.

Department of the Interior: Bureau of Commercial Fisheries
(Fisheries Attaches)

Functions. Fisheries attaches investigate and report on significant commercial fisheries developments. They are interested in the size of the catch, marketing techniques, foreign trade, technical advances, biological studies, and improvements in equipment or vessels. Attaches attend meetings of fisheries associations and may serve as advisers to United States delegates at international conferences dealing with fisheries conventions and trade and conservation agreements. They help promote United States trade in fish or fish products by seeking to eliminate trade barriers.

Development and Size. Representatives from the Bureau have served in technical assistance programs. A fisheries representative with a close relationship to the Bureau of Commercial Fisheries has been in

Tokyo most of the time since the end of World War II. This fisheries attache position in Tokyo was eliminated in 1955 as the result of a cut in the budget of the Department of State, but the program was reinstituted in 1957 following pressure from the commercial fisheries industry. A fisheries officer, assigned to Mexico City, has responsibilities in Mexico and all other Latin American countries. In 1961 an attache was appointed to Copenhagen to cover Western Europe and the Soviet Union. In 1962, a new post was approved for West Africa.

Description and Problems. The Bureau of Commercial Fisheries has a major voice in the selection of these attaches. In each instance its recommendations have been accepted by the Department of State. The Bureau also gets information from economic officers at other posts abroad through the Current Economic Reporting Program. This material is useful but, it is said, "some is very good and some not so good." The Bureau is not fully satisfied with the reporting under the Current Economic Reporting Program. Requests for special information not included in the program reporting can be sent to the field, but it normally takes between one and two months to get an answer.

The Bureau does have an opportunity to brief commercial officers before they leave for overseas assignments, but it believes an expansion in the number of fisheries attaches is necessary to provide adequate coverage of expanding world fishery developments. The Department of State, however, sets a low priority on this aspect of overseas work. It has been suggested that the Bureau study the State-Commerce Agreement as a possible pattern of relationship to the Foreign Service. The Bureau is doubtful that any additional funds would be forthcoming if it were to propose its own budget because of the parochial views of the Congressional committees concerned.

The two attaches now overseas were appointed as Foreign Service Reserve officers. The Bureau hopes to establish some form of rotation system, with attaches expected to fit in as area desk officers when they return from overseas. These officers would be entitled to return to their old General Schedule level in the Civil Service. The Bureau has not yet had to face up to the rotation problem.

Future Requirements. The Bureau hopes to add an attache in 1964 for better service in South America. By 1965, it wants to have attaches for North and East Africa. While all these attaches are needed now, according to a Bureau representative, to be practical, priorities have been set as to the representation that can realistically be requested.

41

PROPOSED AND NEW PROGRAMS

Department of Health, Education, and Welfare: Office of Education
(Educational Attaches) [12]

Functions. The Office of Education has proposed that educational attaches be assigned to embassies. A function of educational attaches would be the gathering of information abroad on educational matters of interest to federal, state, and private educational officials. An educational attache system would be a logical recognition of the growing importance of education as a necessary foundation for economic and social development.

Attaches would provide information that would assist United States educators to understand foreign cultures so that American patterns of education could be satisfactorily adjusted before being applied to the reorganization of United States educational programs in underdeveloped countries. Attaches would also be expected to serve as specialized contacts to bring together foreign and United States educators. With the increasing emphasis on educational matters in our foreign relations, educational attaches would be valuable as policy advisers to the ambassadors and as reporting officers for the Department of State.

Size and Development. The program has not yet become a reality. The need for educational attaches and a description of their function has been a matter of continuing discussion over a period of years. The number of attaches suggested has varied from two to twelve depending largely upon the extent to which the suggestion is considered to be a pilot project.

Description and Problems. The principal objection to educational attaches is that their functions would be a duplication of those of United States Information Service (USIS) officers and AID education advisers overseas. If the United States is to meet satisfactorily the requirements of today's world, close professional contacts with foreign educational leaders and officials are important. The United States probably does need complete and frequent reports on educational developments abroad—a continuing appraisal of the effects of foreign influences on the education of any given country. The United States must also disseminate information about its educational system—not only its advantages but its shortcomings as well.

---

[12] The Social Security Administration will also have an interest in the social welfare attache program, the exact nature of which will depend on the relationships worked out between the Social Security Administration and the Welfare Administration regarding the program.

42

The manner in which these goals are accomplished is immaterial. The USIS can staff its overseas missions with qualified, experienced cultural officers who have the necessary educational background and status to enable them to meet foreign educational leaders on an equal footing. If, however, USIS cannot supply the qualified personnel and the required man-hours, then the need for special educational attaches remains.

Future Requirements. The persons interviewed were necessarily vague on what the future requirements might be. They were interested in getting the program under way. If agreement can be reached between the Department of Health, Education, and Welfare and the Department of State, no more than two such attaches will be named in the near future. After that, a slow growth is likely.

Department of Health, Education, and Welfare: Vocational Rehabilitation Administration (Vocational Rehabilitation Attaches)

Functions. The Vocational Rehabilitation Administration has proposed that vocational rehabilitation attaches be assigned to selected embassies. The functions of these attaches have not yet been spelled out. It appears, however, that a major function might be the administration of the VRA's foreign research program established under P.L. 480. They might assist in the rehabilitation research exchange of American and foreign experts under P.L. 610—the International Health Research Act. They might also help in the selection of persons interested in vocational rehabilitation for exchange under the other United States and international programs. They might also gather information from abroad relating to research in rehabilitation or other programs being conducted in the United States by the VRA. They could attend international conferences in their areas on vocational rehabilitation matters, and furnish information from abroad to be used in the preparation of United States policy at such conferences.

Size and Development. The question of sending such attaches abroad has not progressed beyond several informal discussions with the Department of State. The Department of Health, Education, and Welfare has had an interest in international vocational rehabilitation activities since 1947. In 1955, a domestic research program aimed at finding better ways to rehabilitate disabled persons was initiated. In 1960, research activities were extended to include foreign countries, utilizing P.L. 480 local currencies, and with research being done by foreign nationals. During the first two years of this program,

43

twenty-five research projects in six countries—Brazil, Burma, India, Israel, Pakistan, and Egypt—were undertaken. In Indonesia, Poland, Syria, and Yugoslavia, agricultural counterpart funds are available for this purpose when they are in excess of United States embassy and other primary United States requirements. Although cooperating agencies in the foreign countries are asked to identify their own major problems and the areas in which they are most competent to do research, projects approved must also help meet problems the United States is facing in the field.

Problems. Other agencies now have personnel overseas servicing P.L. 480 foreign research programs, but the question as to whether such personnel should or should not be attaches or be members of the Foreign Service or Foreign Service Reserve is still unsettled. In 1962, the Department of State ruled that personnel administering a P.L. 480 foreign research program could no longer be designated as assistant science attaches and have diplomatic status if their work were limited to carrying out a domestic assignment. If work were done for the ambassador or the Department of State in addition to duties performed for domestic purposes, an individual could be appointed to the Foreign Service Reserve by the State Department with reimbursement for his Reserve salary and allowances from the domestic agency concerned.

Future Requirements. In the event an attache program of this kind is approved, it will probably be started on a small experimental basis with no more than one or two such personnel overseas—possibly with one representative to service the Near East and South Asia area. Any further expansion will depend upon the proven value of the attaches to the VRA, to the United States embassies they service, and to the Department of State's policymaking or representational activities.

Department of Health, Education, and Welfare: Welfare Administration (Social Welfare Attaches)

Functions. The functions of the recently reinstituted social welfare attache category, dormant from 1952 to 1963, include reporting on overseas social conditions and indicating the effects of social development on political and economic affairs. Attaches analyze the social welfare programs that have been established, the social needs, and how well the programs are meeting needs. The information will be useful to the ambassador in coordinating policy implementation. Welfare administration officials believe this program will give a new

44

dimension to policy formulation in the Department of State, because general reporting on social welfare developments has lacked specialized perception. Furthermore, it is hoped that social welfare attaches will explain United States welfare programs to foreign specialists in a better manner than is possible for regular Foreign Service officers or for the "generalists" in USIS. According to Welfare Administration representatives, few welfare leaders abroad now understand what is being accomplished in the United States in the social welfare field.

Size and Development. A social welfare attache program did exist from 1948 to 1952, with attaches in Paris and New Delhi, but budget cuts eliminated the attaches. Apparently State Department reaction to the proposal to revive the program was mixed. Most enthusiastic was the Bureau of African Affairs. The term social welfare unfortunately has a bad connotation to certain individuals, including some ambassadors. Work is continuing on the determination of the specific functions of such attaches, and selected embassies have been asked to express their attitudes about the usefulness of personnel performing social welfare functions. One social welfare attache has already been appointed to the United States embassy staff in Rio de Janeiro.

NON-ATTACHE-TYPE
PROGRAMS

PROGRAMS WITH FUNCTIONS primarily of a non-attache type that for the most part do not require attache services are discussed here under three major headings: (1) Regulatory and Control Programs, (2) Research Programs, and (3) Other Administrative or Operational Programs. Research programs may be subdivided into two types: research programs abroad carried on for domestic purposes by personnel of domestic agencies, and research programs administered abroad under P.L. 480 by foreign personnel for domestic purposes. Although most of the programs to be subsumed under the above headings appear appropriately placed, it will be noted that legal attaches who are special agents of the Federal Bureau of Investigation (FBI) are classified as performing regulatory and control functions despite their attache title.

Among the personnel surveyed who are listed as performing functions related to regulation and control activities essentially for domestic purposes are: (a) the overseas inspectors of the Agricultural Research Service of the Department of Agriculture; (b) the overseas personnel of the Flight Standards Service of the Federal Aviation Agency; (c) the medical officers of the Division of Foreign Quarantine of the National Institutes of Health of the Department of Health, Education, and Welfare; (d) the legal attaches of the FBI of the

47

Department of Justice; (*e*) the immigration officers of the Immigration and Naturalization Service of the Department of Justice; (*f*) the customs and narcotics agents of the Bureau of Customs and the Bureau of Narcotics of the Department of the Treasury; and (*g*) the internal revenue agents of the Bureau of Internal Revenue of the Department of the Treasury.

Personnel in a separate category engaged in research programs are the entomologists of the Agricultural Research Service of the Department of Agriculture. These entomologists carry out research projects at overseas locations designed to improve the control of certain pests which might threaten American agriculture if they should spread to the United States, or conduct research on insects, predators, and parasites which might be introduced into the United States to help control American pests or unwanted plant growths. The function of these entomologists is quite different from that of the overseas inspectors of the Agricultural Research Service, although the long-range purpose is much the same.

The administration and servicing of programs of domestic affairs agencies falls to the personnel who direct the P.L. 480 research programs for both the Agricultural Research Service of the Department of Agriculture and the National Institutes of Health of the Department of Health, Education, and Welfare. These personnel, operating under separate personnel systems and in different fields of research, administer research programs by foreign nationals financed by foreign currencies through the sale of excess agricultural products under P.L. 480. Other administrative or operational programs are the station managers and technical representatives of the National Aeronautics and Space Administration, who have responsibility for overseas tracking facilities used by the space agency.

REGULATORY AND CONTROL PROGRAMS

Department of Agriculture: Agricultural Research Service
(Regulation and Control)

Functions. Personnel from the Agricultural Research Service are stationed in foreign countries to watch for outbreaks of animal diseases or insect pests. They do no research, but make inspections and report on outbreaks which might threaten American agriculture. They become familiar with particular problems in the areas of their assignment and, in some instances, may assist in the control of diseases or pests.

Size and Development. Twenty-eight Civil Service employees of the Department of Agriculture are now performing these functions. Three

48

are serving with the Mexican-United States Joint Commission on Hoof and Mouth Disease. One man is assigned in The Netherlands to observe the preparation of bulbs for shipment and to inspect shipments; another makes preshipment inspections in Bermuda; a third performs a similar function in Nassau. About twenty Department of Agriculture employees operate a plant-control center at Monterrey, Mexico, to fight the spread of citrus black fly. In addition, a trained veterinarian is now stationed in Rome to become familiar with the livestock problems of Europe and the Middle East, to exchange information on animal disease outbreaks, and in particular to learn what is being done about African swine and horse fever.

Description. Since all of these operations are relatively small, there is no formal pattern of operation. Personnel are normally assigned for a two-year period, with rotation back to the Department's Agricultural Research Service. However, some individuals enjoy these assignments and may stay for relatively long periods of time. It is hoped to limit such assignments in the future to three two-year periods, with home leave between tours of duty, followed by a post in Washington before further assignment overseas. The personnel remain on the rolls of the Agricultural Research Service and are paid directly by the Department of Agriculture.

Future Requirements. Over a five-year period, requirements are not expected to vary by more than one man. If there were a serious outbreak of a disease or pest, the numbers might be doubled or tripled; funds are available for staff to meet such emergencies.

Federal Aviation Agency: Flight Standards Service
(Aviation Safety Officers and Facilities Flight Inspection Personnel)

Functions. Federal Aviation Agency (FAA) Safety officers and Facilities Inspection personnel serve American commercial and military aviation in fundamentally the same way as the Flight Standards Service does in the United States, but with greater emphasis on facilities and services provided by foreign interests. This includes inspections of aircraft, flight personnel, facilities for getting to and from airports and at airports, and facilities used by United States flag air carriers. These inspections have frequently resulted in improvements in the implementation of facilities as well as conformance with international standards.

Development and Size. The International Division of the Flight Standards Service, including the Washington headquarters and three domestic international field offices in the United States, employs sixty-nine persons in the United States and sixty-four overseas. Eighteen locally recruited clerical personnel and chauffeurs are also employed overseas.

Description and Problems. The Flight Standards Service personnel system overseas has been run on a fairly regular Civil Service basis. The personnel remain on Civil Service appointments during their overseas tours. There are two distinct categories of personnel: one based on the availability of domestic assignments in the International Division in the appropriate grade levels and the other on skill specialties of personnel returning from overseas assignments. For example, the electronics and pilot personnel concerned with the facilities flight check program abroad must be drawn from the Agency's domestic regional offices and, on completion of their overseas duty, return to the positions they left or to similar positions, generally in the same location. Administrative re-employment rights guarantee this. Such an approach is necessary because the International Division of the Flight Standards Service has no counterpart in its field activities within the United States to its facilities flight check functions abroad, and must draw the personnel required for this program from the FAA regions and return them on completion of their two- to four-year tours.

On the other hand, the Aviation Safety officers (including inspectors in aircraft operations, maintenance, and electronics specialties) have a fairly self-contained rotation system within the International Division, since the Division has both domestic and overseas offices with positions appropriate for the grade level and skills used. There is some administrative difficulty in maintaining the rotation system because of: (1) an insufficient number of domestic posts at the GS-14 level (which is equivalent to the level of the heads of the field offices) to match the excessively large number of overseas field offices; (2) disparity between the domestic and overseas programs in the skills needed; (3) problems of obtaining medical clearances for overseas service since, over a period of time, the Division tends to accumulate a number of people who, while still qualifying for Civil Service duties, fail to meet the rigorous physical requirements for State Department medical clearance for overseas service. These problems have on occasion necessitated keeping people overseas beyond the normal two- to four-year period and the recruiting of additional personnel from the regions.

Although it is not believed in Washington that FAA representatives overseas need diplomatic passports, hope was expressed that some of the privileges available to Foreign Service personnel could be made available to FAA personnel on a more uniform basis.[1]

There is a need for language training for overseas personnel. It can sometimes be arranged for after arrival at the overseas post, but prior to departure from the domestic assignment there is generally a lack of funds and time available for training.

Future Requirements. No significant expansion is expected in Flight Standards Service overseas programs in the immediate future, except the FAA assumption of responsibility for flight inspections of military air navigation aids under Project Friendship.[2] Under this program between 100 and 120 Federal Aviation Agency employees will eventually serve as flight inspectors in Frankfurt, Beirut, Manila, and possibly Tokyo. Originally a total of 3,500 to 4,000 FAA employees were expected to go abroad under Project Friendship to perform a variety of flight-control functions now handled by military personnel. Further study on implementing the broader aspects of Project Friendship is required if difficult administrative problems are to be overcome.

Department of Health, Education, and Welfare: Public Health Service, Bureau of Medical Services (Division of Foreign Quarantine)

Functions. Medical officers of the Division of Foreign Quarantine examine visa applicants abroad in accordance with the immigration laws of the United States. When none is stationed in an area, the examinations are done by a physician selected by the applicant from a panel approved by the Department of State. Determining the physical and mental health of an alien who applies for a visa has two benefits: it helps to keep dangerous communicable diseases from being brought into the country; it guards against an alien becoming a public charge because of some physical or mental defect. The alien benefits because it almost completely eliminates the possibility that he will be deported for medical reasons upon arrival in the United States.

Size and Description. There are twenty-nine examining units at most of the large posts in Europe, Canada, Mexico, and Hong Kong, which issue visas and process the majority of immigrants to the United

---

[1] One problem for Civil Service personnel serving overseas has been the high duties imposed on automobiles imported from the United States for private use.

[2] Project Friendship is a proposed agreement between the FAA and the Department of Defense under which FAA civilian employees would replace Department of Defense military employees in the performance of certain inspection and control functions related to military air operations in foreign countries.

51

States. These units at embassies or consulates are staffed by approximately seventy persons, mostly Public Health Service commissioned officers and local physicians employed by the Service. In 1962, these physicians examined more than 189,000 visa applicants. About 130,-000 additional applicants were examined by local Department of Health panel physicians. At the request of the Department, Public Health Service medical officers provide consultative supervision of panel physicians in some parts of Europe, Canada, Mexico, and Hong Kong. In 1963 the Division of Foreign Quarantine set up an additional examination and supervisory office to serve the Caribbean and Central American region. For each alien medical examination performed by a Public Health Service physician, the Department of State collects a fee of $10.00 from the visa applicant. These fees produce enough revenue to cover the cost of the program.

Future Requirements. The medical examination program continues to grow as a result of new exchange programs, increased immigration from unrestricted areas, and immigration under special legislation, such as that covering refugees and escapees. There is a need for expanded consultative supervision of local panel physicians who examine applicants for visas to enter the United States. The Division of Foreign Quarantine foresees about a five to ten per cent growth in the number of its overseas employees each year to keep up with the demand.

Department of Justice: Federal Bureau of Investigation
(Legal Attaches)

Functions. The primary function of legal attaches is to carry out liaison activities overseas related to the domestic responsibility of the FBI in over 165 categories in both the criminal and security fields. They deal with local law enforcement agencies on matters of mutual interest and with local representatives of other United States agencies. Their work overseas does not conflict with any of the delimitation agreements among the agencies considered to be members of the intelligence community.

Development, Size, and Qualifications. Special agents of the FBI were first assigned overseas as legal attaches as early as 1942. As World War II ended, criminal elements familiar with the war-torn areas moved in to take advantage of the postwar chaos. In response, the FBI sent special agents to additional countries. They were attached to the embassies as legal attaches and had diplomatic status. At present liaison posts exist in Paris, London, Rome, Tokyo, Manila, Rio de Janeiro, Bern, Bonn, Madrid, Ottawa, and Mexico City. The practice of according diplomatic status has continued.

Thirty-five special agents with a clerical staff of thirty-six are now serving overseas. Sixteen of the special agents are assigned in Mexico to deal with problems stemming from Mexico's common border with the United States. Although two or three legal attaches are assigned to embassies in London, Paris, and Rome, most of the other posts are manned by one attache.

In addition to the academic background required of special agents, personnel assigned as legal attaches may be specialists in a field or have skill in a foreign language. FBI special agents are not sent overseas until they have had at least five years of successful experience in domestic assignments and have demonstrated particular ability to carry out the duties inherent in the foreign assignments.

Description and Problems. Special agents are not recruited expressly for overseas service but are selected from the FBI's 6,000-member staff of special agents. To be recruited into the FBI, they must be between the ages of twenty-three and forty-one. Only experienced agents who are considered to be exceptionally well-adjusted are later considered for overseas assignments. If knowledge of a particular foreign language is required, the special agent competent in that language is selected. The FBI has had no problems in finding men with adequate language skills for overseas duty.

Special agents accepting assignment abroad as legal attaches agree to serve no less than two years overseas; if their performance has been satisfactory, if there is a continuing need for their services, and if they desire to remain abroad, they may sign for an additional tour. They may indicate their preferences for assignment either at home or abroad at any time. The FBI has had no difficulty in finding capable special agents for overseas duty from among those who express a preference for foreign assignment.

Legal attaches are normally selected at the GS-13 [3] level from the field investigative staff or from the GS-14 level supervisory positions. If they are given supervisory positions overseas, they may be promoted but must revert to their normal grade level upon return unless they are placed in a domestic supervisory position. There has been no problem to date in continuing them in the grade level they achieved overseas. Service abroad is regarded as a step up in the

---

[3] Although the General Schedule grade corresponds to Civil Service terminology, FBI special agents are members of an "excepted service."

Bureau's executive development program. Accordingly, the opportunity to serve abroad often proves beneficial to careers.

During overseas service, a special agent serving as the lone FBI representative at a post, or as the designated head when more than one are assigned, is returned to the United States annually for three-day conferences. Every second year the return includes home leave and every fourth year the return includes a two-week course on investigative techniques and current responsibilities of the FBI. Other special agents serving overseas are returned at least once every two years for conferences and home leave; the return every fourth year includes the two-week course. Inspectors from the FBI visit each post once a year. Although it would be possible for an agent to be reassigned continuously overseas and to make a career of service abroad, none has actually been assigned in this manner.

Legal attaches serve under the general jurisdiction of the ambassador, but they do not clear communications to or from the FBI through the ambassador. Legal attaches are under instructions to report any information to the ambassador and also to send a report for transmittal to the Department of State if they encounter anything the ambassador or the Department of State might find useful. The FBI feels the legal attaches need the diplomatic status accorded them to enable them to perform their overseas functions effectively.

Future Requirements. No increase in the number of legal attaches abroad is anticipated. A review of the needs at each post is made every six months. Additional special agents would be assigned overseas only to meet an essential need relating to the fulfillment of the FBI's domestic responsibilities and only after approval of the State Department.

Department of Justice: Immigration and Naturalization Service (Immigration Officers)

Functions. Most immigration officers are stationed at ports of entry or at offices in the United States. Those stationed abroad not only perform various functions in the administration of immigration laws, but are expected to facilitate travel to and from the United States. Their duties also include the approving of visa petitions that grant the foreign wives of United States citizens immigration status outside the normal quota for the country. Since 1957, they have been authorized to interrogate aliens abroad to determine on behalf of the Attorney General if a waiver of inadmissibility should be issued to an alien who fails to meet entrance requirements. Since 1960, immigration officers have been particularly active in expediting the entry of European refugees into the United States under the liberalized quotas. They also have been responsible for arranging for the immigration of orphan children to the United States for adoption. At certain posts near the United States, inspections are made before air travellers depart in order to speed up entry when they arrive in this country.

Development, Size, and Qualifications. Aliens seeking admission to the United States normally must obtain a visa from a consular officer of the Foreign Service and later, at a port of entry, be approved by an immigration officer of the Justice Department's Immigration and Naturalization Service. Thus, the Departments of State and Justice share responsibility for admission of aliens to the United States. Both test the alien desiring admission on thirty-one counts of inadmissibility.

Shortly after the passage of the Immigration Act of 1924, immigration officers from the Immigration Bureau of the Department of Labor were sent overseas as technical advisers to consular officers.[4] This type of staffing was eliminated in 1939 when immigration slowed down and consular officers became better trained in the technical aspects of administering immigration requirements. It was under Reorganization Plan No. 5 of 1940 that the immigration function was transferred from the Department of Labor and placed in the Immigration and Naturalization Service of the Department of Justice.

As a result of the Displaced Persons Act of 1948 an administrative agreement was reached whereby immigration officers were sent overseas to conduct inspections. An independent Displaced Persons Commission to help select European refugees displaced by World War II was cooperating with the International Refugee Organization in Geneva. Rather than have its selections rejected by immigration officials after arrival in the United States, twelve immigration inspectors were sent overseas to conduct the inspections that would otherwise have been done after arrival. This activity was written into the Refugee Relief Act of 1953. When the Act expired for all practical purposes, the Immigration and Naturalization Service kept two inspectors in Frankfurt to adjudicate visa petitions for wives of American citizens.

After legislation was passed in 1957 giving the Attorney General the right to waive certain standards of inadmissibility for aliens seek-

---

[4] Between the passage, on May 19, 1921, of the first act that established immigration quotas and May 26, 1924, quotas were filled on a first-come first-served basis at the port of entry; each month immigration ships hovered off American ports ready to race ashore to win the quota allotments for their passengers, many of whom did not qualify for admission. The issuance of immigration visas abroad was begun by consular officers in 1924.

ing to come to the United States, the Immigration and Naturalization Service by agreement with the Department of State established overseas representation at Frankfurt, Vienna, Rome, Naples, Athens, Havana, Tokyo, Hong Kong, and Manila. (In 1960, the Havana office was closed, and an office was opened in Palermo.)

The offices are staffed by twenty-two immigration officers and a secretarial staff of over thirty. In addition, pre-inspection offices for persons traveling to the United States have been opened in Vancouver, Winnipeg, Montreal, and Toronto, Canada; in Hamilton, Bermuda; in Nassau, Bahamas; and in Mexico City. These offices are staffed by thirty-five immigration officers and two clerical assistants.

Officers assigned overseas normally have had varied experiences as members of the Border Patrol, port of entry inspectors, adjudicators on applications for admission, naturalization examiners, or investigators. An ability to speak a foreign language is desired but not required.

Description and Problems. Original employment by the Immigration and Naturalization Service is primarily for domestic purposes, and all new officer employees serve first in the Border Patrol, entering at the GS-7 level and spending from one to three years on assignment to the Patrol. Emphasized in the orientation following entry into the Service are the Spanish language, an understanding of the Immigration and Naturalization Service and the laws it enforces, and the handling of firearms.

The Service has a college recruitment program designed to attract college seniors. New recruits, however, average about two and one-half years of college education.

Both officers and clerks serve overseas for a single two-year period, with the possibility of extending the tour for one additional year. At the end of three years at most, the overseas employees are returned from abroad for assignment in the United States. The Service's policy is to rotate as many of its better young officers overseas as possible, believing that overseas service helps them gain a rounded background. There has been no problem of reassigning returning immigration officers to positions in the United States at the job levels they have held overseas and there has been no difficulty in finding applicants for overseas duty.

Immigration officers work closely with State Department officials, particularly the consular officers. Although the Service's personnel abroad are under the general jurisdiction of the ambassador, all technical direction of their work comes from the Immigration and Naturalization Service.

Future Requirements. The role of the Immigration and Naturalization Service overseas depends exclusively upon legislative authorization. Personnel requirements—both as to numbers and type—would have to be determined in the development of any legislation, but the Service believes it would have no difficulty in staffing any conceivable program related to its area of responsibility from among its employees.

Department of the Treasury: Bureau of Customs
(Customs Agents and Customs Representatives)

Development and Size. The Division of Investigations and Enforcement of the Customs Service, known as the Customs Agency Service, is composed of approximately 250 customs agents and about 520 customs port investigators. All customs port investigators are stationed in the United States; however, approximately twenty customs agents are assigned to foreign posts. Those assigned to foreign posts are designated as United States customs representatives.

On the American continent representatives are stationed in Montreal and Mexico City. A regional customs representative (GS-15), whose headquarters is in Rome, directs all investigative activity throughout Europe, Africa, and the Near East. Sub-offices are situated in Paris, Frankfurt, and London. In the Far East the regional customs representative (GS-14) stationed in Tokyo is responsible for these activities in the Republic of Korea, Japan, Okinawa, the Philippines, Hong Kong, and Singapore.

Functions. Customs representatives abroad conduct a wide range of investigations that include highly technical surveys and developing information leading to the discovery of sources and methods of smuggling into the United States all types of contraband.

One of the essential missions of representatives stationed abroad is the investigation and reporting of data pertaining to the market value, cost of production, classification, marking, undervaluation, false invoicing, and "dumping" of merchandise shipped to the United States. This activity not only provides essential protection against all types of revenue frauds, but it also enables customs officers in the United States to assess duty on legally established bases of accurate appraisement, which ensures the revenue and assists the government in customs court litigations.

In addition, customs representatives overseas serve a vital need in counseling foreign shippers, exporters, manufacturers, trade associations, American buyers, tourists, and government officials in regard to customs requirements, thus contributing to smoothness of international commercial relations and minimizing penalties incurred through inadvertent violations of customs regulations.

Description and Problems. In the Customs Service there is no separate foreign service. Persons stationed abroad usually remain from two to eight years, although there is no maximum period, and several have stayed abroad for more than ten years.

Customs representatives are selected for foreign service on the basis of their background in investigative work, experience, personality, as well as of special qualifications, such as their ability to adapt to living abroad and linguistic capabilities. Wives are also checked for adaptability to conditions of living abroad. The work that customs representatives perform abroad cannot be learned in college. Preparation for it must derive from actual experience in the domestic service. Many customs representatives are bilingual and have had extensive firsthand experience in the use of foreign languages. Usually, agents are selected from the Civil Service Treasury Enforcement Agents registers, qualification for which requires a law degree, training in police administration, or actual law enforcement experience. Promotion is always made on a merit basis as openings occur. Although all agents are subject to transfer within the United States, they are not sent abroad without their prior consent.

Customs representatives assigned abroad are given overseas orientation before departure at the State Department Foreign Service Institute. Upon reaching their assignment, they are given office space in embassies and consulates or in other buildings leased by the Department of State.

Future Requirements. The number of customs representatives stationed abroad is expected to increase in future years; however, this will depend on the volume of world trade and other variable factors. The Bureau of Customs looks at the requirements for overseas representatives on a year-to-year basis and makes adjustment accordingly.

Department of the Treasury: Bureau of Narcotics
(Narcotics Agents)

Functions. The work of narcotics agents is concerned primarily with helping foreign police officials apprehend the persons responsible for the shipment of narcotics destined for the United States. Although the agents do this for domestic purposes, their work may assist foreign officials to control their own problems. Narcotics agents operate under cover, maintaining close relationships with enforcement officials of foreign countries.

Development and Size. Agents have been stationed overseas for about ten years. There are ten employees at the officer level, and five at the secretarial level. Agents are selected for their investigative ability.

Description and Problems. Most agents are first selected at GS-11 or GS-12 level for an overseas assignment. They normally go abroad for two-year assignments. There is no difficulty in absorbing them back into posts in the United States; they are normally reassigned to do work related to their overseas assignment. Agents are selected from a field office and returned to a field office.

Although they do work under cover, agents have office space provided by the Department of State in eight cities overseas, and the Bureau of Narcotics reimburses the Department of State for administrative services. Agents are cleared with both the State Department and with foreign enforcement agencies before being sent overseas. Overseas agents work closely with FBI and customs agents.

Only the best narcotics agents are sent overseas. After studying police administration in college, most of the agents start their first job for the Bureau of Narcotics at one of the thirteen United States district offices. Since the work of the Bureau is very specialized, they usually plan to make service with the Bureau a career.

Future Requirements. It is expected that as additional responsibilities arise there will be some growth in the number of agents stationed overseas in coming years. As the work of agents becomes better known and increasingly accepted by other governments, personnel requirements will probably increase. Actually, when the narcotics trade is closed down in one area, agents can be moved to other places. Suppliers tend to close one operation and move to another location. The narcotics agents are never far behind.

Department of the Treasury: Internal Revenue Service (Revenue Service Representatives)

Functions. Revenue Service representatives and their staff stationed abroad are high-level technicians—internal revenue agents—who give assistance to United States taxpayers (citizen or alien) in fulfilling their tax obligations. To achieve this they work with their counterparts in foreign countries under terms established in tax treaties; they supply information concerning such problems to the Treasury Department officials who negotiate the tax treaties. Their job is to protect United States taxpayers from double taxation, which stems from differences in tax philosophies. United States income, estate, and gift tax laws apply to its citizens throughout the world, but many other countries use the source rule in taxation. The representatives also help enforce tax liabilities. Since citizenship is a basis of the United States tax system, attention is also given to determining the areas where citizens are concentrated abroad, so that they may be provided with adequate information and assistance.

Development and Size. The first overseas office of the Internal Revenue Service was established in Manila in 1936. Two years later an office was opened in Paris and the next year in London. The outbreak of the war in Europe forced the closing of the Paris and London offices in 1939; the Manila office was closed in 1941, just before the attack on Pearl Harbor. The Paris office was reopened in 1948, and additional offices were opened early in 1956 at Frankfurt, Ottawa, and Manila. The Frankfurt office was closed and a new one established in London in 1958. A South American office was opened in São Paulo in 1960, and an office for Central America in Mexico City in 1962.

Twelve agents and six clerical employees are now assigned overseas. In addition to these, during the period that taxes are filed, eighteen to twenty agents are overseas temporarily. They visit embassies and consulates to help United States taxpayers and military posts to give tax instruction to members of the Judge Advocate General Corps.

Description and Problems. The Internal Revenue Service totals some 58,000 employees in the Washington office, sixty-two districts, and nine regions in the United States. Agents selected for overseas service are recruited from the districts. At least three years' service in the field examining income tax returns is required before consideration for overseas assignment. Experience in fraud, appellate, and collection work, as well as in auditing, is desirable. Knowledge of a foreign language is considered in selection. Once chosen, the agents are required to agree to remain abroad for two full years; this may be extended to not more than five years. Home leave may be taken upon agreement to return abroad. These agents are brought to Washington for training in overseas aspects of the Internal Revenue Code. If required, training in a foreign language is arranged at the

Foreign Service Institute Language School. Agents assigned abroad for the first time usually are given the second or third ranking position at the post, as a grade GS-12 or GS-13. Upon completion of an overseas assignment, the agent may be reassigned to the Washington office or to one of the districts and, after one year or more, may be considered for another overseas assignment.

There is no problem in finding agents who are willing to accept assignment abroad, but not all who apply can meet the exacting requirements. Married men at least twenty-six years of age and having unusual ability to meet and deal with persons of wealth and position (both citizen and alien), as well as having a broad knowledge of the Internal Revenue law and procedure are preferred. In the future it is likely that personnel will be assigned first to a less desirable post so that the possibility of a better assignment can be held out as an inducement to the acceptance of the less desirable first assignment.

Agents assigned to the lower ranking positions may aspire to the GS-14 level and, if they become Revenue Service representatives, to GS-15. When higher ranking men return to this country it is difficult to find them jobs of comparable level. Thus, personnel may be given temporary appointments overseas at higher levels and may be expected to revert to their old grade levels when they return.

Revenue Service representatives are given diplomatic status, but for various reasons not all of them are on the diplomatic list.[5] Generally, they are not involved in activities requiring the expenditure of representation allowances. The placement of Revenue Service representatives overseas must be negotiated through the Department of State with the country in which the post is to be located.

Some officials of the Internal Revenue Service are working toward the concept of a career service. With forty agents abroad they believe such a service would be workable, and could be accomplished through close cooperation of the Treasury Department and the Department of State.

Future Requirements. Additional overseas offices may be opened in Rome, Frankfurt, and Tokyo—and other cities have been under study—along with budget estimates for them. It is not anticipated that there will ever be a need for more than forty agents overseas on permanent assignment.

---

[5] A diplomatic list is generally issued several times a year by a receiving government and includes the name of each individual with diplomatic status who is accredited to the country, his job title, telephone number, home address, and whether he has a wife or children of age. The name of the senior member of each embassy is listed in order of precedence, with the date of presentation of credentials.

RESEARCH PROGRAMS

Department of Agriculture: Agricultural Research Service
(American Research Abroad)

Functions. Selected employees of the Agriculture Research Service are stationed in foreign countries to do research on insects, predators, and parasites which might either threaten American agriculture or be introduced into the United States to help control pests that damage livestock or plants. The individuals doing this research are generally professional entomologists.

Size and Development. There are twenty-one American professional employees and a supporting staff engaged in this program. Seventeen professionals are working overseas for the Entomology Research Division conducting projects in the following locations: Paris, Rome, Rabat, Mexico City, Buenos Aires, and on the islands of Grand Turk, Mayaguana, and San Salvador. One researcher is studying hoof and mouth disease in Amsterdam, and three have been assigned to Kenya to study African swine fever.

Description. Assignments are normally for two-year periods followed by home leave. It is not felt that the researchers lose their specialties by this assignment, since they are using their techniques daily, although they may not learn about advances being made in the United States. It is anticipated that researchers will not be kept in the field for more than three two-year assignments in succession. Some may then return to the Agricultural Research Division permanently; others, who speak a foreign language or like living abroad, may be reassigned overseas after two years of reorientation in the Department.

Future Requirements. The number of personnel required for overseas service is not expected to vary by more than one or two men over a five-year period. Funds are available, however, for quick expansion in the event of serious outbreaks that would need to be studied.

Department of Agriculture: Agricultural Research Service
(P.L. 480 Foreign Research)

Functions. Some employees of the Agriculture Research Service are stationed overseas to administer foreign agricultural research programs financed by foreign currencies through the sale of excess agricultural products under P.L. 480. Although they work through agricultural attaches, they may negotiate the technical aspects of research projects with the ministry of agriculture or health of a foreign

62

government and, through that ministry, ascertain what local institution—private or public—should conduct a particular research job. While this research must be in the domestic interest of the United States in order to be justified, it can actually benefit both nations involved and often has long-range foreign affairs implications. In addition to servicing the needs of the Agricultural Research Service, these personnel also administer research programs of interest to the Economic Research Service, the Forest Service, and the Marketing Research Service.

Size and Development. Programs are now being conducted in twenty-five countries of Europe, Asia, and Latin America. Two field offices are maintained—one in Rome and the other in New Delhi—staffed by Civil Service employees of the Agricultural Research Service. In Rome there are two professionals, two administrators, two clerical employees, as well as local employees. In New Delhi there are two professionals, one administrator, and one administrative assistant, in addition to locally recruited staff. The Latin American program is serviced from Washington, but with difficulty. Non-technical portions of the work are done with the assistance of agricultural attaches. Qualifications required of personnel are a background of research in the physical sciences, and the facility to deal with all kinds of people.

Description. Personnel are recruited from the Civil Service employees of the Agricultural Research Service. It is hoped that their term of service will be for no more than three two-year tours of duty abroad before they return to the Department for two years of reorientation. The Agricultural Research Service is now recruiting personnel for these positions with the idea that they can make a career of this kind of work. Recruits are "guaranteed" that when they return to jobs in the Department they will retain the same job level they held in the field.

Professional personnel have hitherto had diplomatic status, but it has been indicated that the Department of State may now question this practice on the ground that their work is primarily "the extension of a domestic activity" which does not require for its success the social status of being on the diplomatic list. Even if the program's purpose is domestic, the Department of Agriculture argues that these personnel need the benefits that derive from possession of this status.[6]

---

[6] For example, if a new car is imported into India by a person without diplomatic status, a 150 per cent import tax must be paid. Some of this tax can be recovered upon departure, but, it is said, few of Agriculture's personnel can afford to borrow this amount for the period of service.

There is also some concern in the Agriculture Department that the top level of the Foreign Service pay scale is much higher than that currently authorized for its employees. The P.L. 480 program recruits at the GS-13 or GS-14 level, but the Department believes the responsibilities of the job should entitle its overseas employees to GS-16 or GS-17 ratings.

All four services of the Department of Agriculture being served are informed of staff openings. For a single position, the program had twenty-three applicants.

Future Requirements. At present, the only possibility of an additional field office is one to service Latin America. It would require no more than four to six United States citizen employees.

Department of Health, Education, and Welfare: National Institutes of Health (P.L. 480 Foreign Research Program)

Functions. The National Institutes of Health were established to carry out and support "biomedical" research and training that would further the improvement of the general health of the American people. Thus, the international activities of the NIH are fundamentally overseas extensions of domestic programs and missions. Such activities include research and training grants to foreign institutions and international organizations, stipends for foreign nationals to come to the United States or for Americans to go abroad for research and training, and contracts and collaborative research projects with foreign institutions. Approximately $30,000,000 was expended in 1962 for these various activities. Personnel assigned to the P.L. 480 foreign research program have been responsible for administering research grants disbursed in foreign currencies by income received through the sale of agricultural surplus commodities. Under this program, research of benefit to the United States is carried on abroad by foreign nationals.

Personnel assigned to overseas offices are responsible for maintaining liaison with scientists, research institutions, and national scientific bodies within each pertinent geographic area, and for providing assistance, information, and advice to the NIH, to the foreign contacts, and to overseas representatives of other United States government agencies especially with regard to the NIH programs and policies. These personnel furnish the NIH with information on scientific interests, capabilities, and resources available overseas and evaluate information on longer ranger scientific trends in biomedicine in terms of possible effects on the NIH program planning. They also alert

64

the Institutes to special research opportunities which might otherwise be unknown, help develop project proposals, and serve as official representatives of the NIH at biomedical conferences and international meetings.

Development and Size. In response to the increasing responsibilities of the Institutes for studying, planning, and conducting its international activities, the Office of International Research was established in 1961 as part of the Office of the Director of the NIH; through this office the Institutes' personnel are assigned overseas. The personnel are not part of any NIH personnel program designed specifically to train and recruit people for overseas assignments; they are highly accomplished scientists and administrators who have special qualifications for overseas duty and are generally drawn from the professional ranks at the Institutes.

In addition to these representatives, the NIH also maintain laboratories overseas and assign professional personnel to them to conduct specific research programs at the Institutes.[7] Recently three different overseas offices have been established by the Office of International Research, in large part to assist in the conduct of the foreign research program: a European Office in Paris, a Pacific Office in Tokyo, and a Latin American Office in Rio de Janeiro. A science representative serves in London under the European Office; a similar representative is in New Delhi for the Pacific Office.

Nineteen persons are assigned to these offices; seven may be regarded as professional scientist administrators and the remaining twelve as administrative officers and secretarial staff.

Description and Problems. Personnel staffing the overseas offices are employed by the Office of International Research of the NIH. They are either Civil Service employees or members of the Public Health Service Commissioned Officer Corps. All of the overseas offices are in quarters rented by the American embassy, and in each case the embassy is reimbursed by the Office of International Research for office space and general administrative and overhead costs incurred in the operation of the overseas office.

Because the overseas offices have only recently been formed, the NIH have faced few personnel problems other than those involved in the initial transporting of staff, establishing actual office operations, and making foreign contacts.

Future Requirements. The Institutes currently have about ten scien-

---

[7] Their activities were not studied, although the number of personnel involved is apparently larger than in the P.L. 480 foreign research program.

tists in training for the administration of research programs overseas and expect to have ten to fifteen additional scientists working overseas within the next two years.

OTHER ADMINISTRATIVE OR OPERATIONAL PROGRAMS

National Aeronautics and Space Administration: Office of International Programs and Office of Tracking and Data Acquisition (Station Managers and Technical Representatives)

Representatives of the National Aeronautics and Space Administration have served tours of duty at overseas stations since 1959 in support of NASA programs that required the staffing of a minitrack network, a Mercury network, deep space instrumentation facilities, and Baker-Nunn optical facilities. Only a few of NASA's representatives abroad—station managers and technical representatives—are on NASA personnel rolls. Most of the Americans serving overseas in NASA programs are on a contract basis. The NASA Office of International Programs is responsible for non-technical aspects of overseas activities. Direct responsibility for network operations is placed in the NASA Office of Tracking and Data Acquisition.

Functions. Station managers serve as the directors of overseas tracking facilities which are under United States management, while technical representatives serve as advisers to tracking facilities in Australia and South Africa managed and operated by local personnel. Station managers are responsible for setting up and operating tracking stations; training local personnel where feasible to assist in station operations; making the station available to the host country for scientific purposes; making data collected by the station available to the host country; maintaining close relations with the scientific community in the host country; and lecturing on space activities. Technical representatives maintain liaison with the local managers, operators, and the scientific community for both technical and public relations purposes. American personnel serving on contract are mostly engineers and technicians—often skilled employees on loan from the firms that have manufactured the tracking equipment.

Development, Size, and Qualifications. When NASA was established in October 1958, it assumed responsibility for several Latin American tracking stations that had already been established by the Office of Naval Research in support of the Vanguard program. NASA now staffs tracking stations in Australia, Bermuda, Canada, Chile, Ecuador, England, Mexico, Nigeria, Peru, South Africa, Zanzibar, and Grand Canary Island. At the end of 1962, NASA's overseas personnel consisted of fifteen station managers and technical representatives serving on its own personnel rolls, 178 American contract personnel, and 416 foreign nationals. There are no station managers or technical representatives stationed in Canada or England, and only technical representatives are sent to Australia and South Africa. From fourteen to thirty-one American personnel serve on contract at each NASA-directed station on a more or less permanent basis, and additional personnel are on short-term assignment during the conduct of a mission. The number of foreign nationals employed at the tracking stations varies from a low of fourteen at one station to over fifty at several locations.

Station managers and technical representatives, in addition to being technically capable of managing network stations and possessing qualities for dealing with the scientific community, must also be able to understand political and cultural problems. Stations are placed in the back country, usually at some distance from the capital city, and require staffing by persons with considerable initiative and ability to deal with the local inhabitants.

The locations of stations were decided by scientists and engineers on the basis of where checkpoints would be needed to track proposed projects. When there was some flexibility on checkpoint areas, the Department of State was consulted about political factors to determine the most favorable locations. Detailed agreements concerning the right to use desired sites were then negotiated by the Department of State with the countries concerned. Agreements are for relatively brief periods and require renegotiation from time to time.

Description and Problems. Senior personnel at GS-14 and GS-15 levels serve as station managers and technical representatives. NASA's problem is to find well-qualified men willing to take their families to isolated hardship posts. The major incentive for personnel who have accepted such posts has been the challenge of the task confronting NASA and the opportunity to be the technical "boss" of a complex operation.

Newly designated station managers or technical representatives are given a brief orientation by the Department of State and the United States Information Agency. They spend several weeks talking with appropriate NASA officials about their supporting role and the equipment they will operate and may be sent to observe the operation of a tracking station for two or three weeks before starting a tour of duty. They are returned to the United States once a year for consultation and briefing. Overseas assignments last two years; extensions thereafter are reviewed on an annual basis. The posts have actually been staffed for only three years, and NASA does not yet have experience with the effect that such service has on specialization, nor how it will influence career development. Certainly overseas service for NASA is not yet viewed as a career in itself.

While the station managers and technical representatives are under the general jurisdiction of the ambassador, they are not closely related to the embassy and are under the technical direction of NASA. They are advised to stay out of political affairs and to avoid political discussions in the country of assignment.

Future Requirements. Staff requirements for NASA in the future will shift as programs change. As programs in support of space activities are expanded the number of NASA personnel overseas will undoubtedly increase, but at the moment the situation is somewhat fluid and no accurate predictions can be made. Personnel officials do not believe it will be too difficult for NASA to provide staff for new facilities from its growing pool of skilled personnel chosen from NASA's 28,-000 employees or by contract from private industry. It is possible that NASA will eventually be able to hire and retain the same kind of employees on its own personnel rolls as are now serving on a contract basis.

It should be noted that the Office of International Programs is responsible for cooperative projects with fifty countries concerning satellites, sounding rockets, and ground-based study of meteorology, communications, and the ionosphere. By January 1963, it also participated in ninety-five exchanges of foreign personnel interested in space activities. NASA is considering assigning a representative to Europe to act as liaison officer for cooperative projects in that area.

IV

ANALYSIS OF
EXISTING
PERSONNEL SYSTEMS

EVEN THOUGH TWENTY-THREE PROGRAMS and personnel systems representing major overseas interests of ten federal domestic agencies have been neatly classified for descriptive purposes as programs with attache-type and non-attache-type functions,[1] such as a presentation is no more than a rather inaccurate map for guiding an exploration of what exists or should exist. Actually, the case may not be clear-cut for including all personnel presently performing reporting, negotiating, and representation functions in the attache category and excluding all personnel engaged in regulation and control, research, and administration or operations. In fact, although scientific representatives of the Atomic Energy Commission perform many of the same functions assigned to attaches, they are not at present automatically classified as attaches by the Department of State.[2] In contrast, legal attaches selected from among the special agents of the FBI carry the title and prerogatives but perform functions largely of a regulatory and controlling nature. Other personnel, such as the proposed vocational rehabilitation attaches, serve multiple functions

---

[1] See Chapters II and III.
[2] Often they serve as a member of a scientific "team" under a Foreign Service Reserve science attache who has a close relationship and responsibility to the Office of International Scientific Affairs of the Department of State.

and have duties that seem to fall under more than one of the analytical categories used here.

From the nature of the functions normally carried out by attache-type personnel, the inference can be drawn that all personnel performing functions with significant foreign affairs impact should be attaches. Do the technically trained representatives of domestic agencies who negotiate with foreign governments or private institutions regarding the technical aspects of grants for research to be conducted overseas by foreign personnel under P.L. 480 funds fall within the attache category under this formula? The grants they administer have considerable impact on the future capabilities of the recipient nation for economic or other development even though they must first be justified solely on the basis of whether they are beneficial to the domestic interest of the United States. Technical personnel of the Flight Standards Service of the Federal Aviation Agency are influential in adjusting standards for handling aircraft en route and at foreign airfields to conform with American and international standards, a process which often requires action by the foreign government concerned. They have been classified here as performing a regulation and control function. Do they fail to qualify as attache-type personnel? This is the present ruling of the Department of State.

The scientific representatives of the Atomic Energy Commission, the legal attaches of the FBI, the proposed vocational rehabilitation attaches of the Department of Health, Education, and Welfare, the directors of the P.L. 480 research programs of the Departments of Agriculture and of Health, Education, and Welfare, and the technical personnel of the Federal Aviation Agency are all examples of personnel groups on the borderline of what are and are not at present considered to be attache services. In part, the problem is one of drawing the line between personnel whose functions are primarily associated with foreign affairs or have considerable impact on foreign affairs and those with functions primarily associated with domestic affairs or having little impact on foreign affairs.

Currently, other factors are also involved. Attaches have diplomatic privileges and immunities that may benefit overseas personnel who have very little impact on foreign affairs—namely legal attaches. Also, attaches are more likely to be included on the diplomatic list and to participate in the social life of a foreign capital than are other overseas personnel. This participation could conceivably be beneficial to personnel conducting a program of purely domestic interest. In addition, diplomatic privileges and immunities are normally granted on a reciprocal basis, with the personnel to be included severely limited by some foreign countries. The United States government must adjust to such variations. Compounding the problem is the fact that if certain categories of American personnel are granted attache status in a particular country overseas, other governments are in a position to request similar privileges in the same country; this increase in number of attaches of other governments may not always be in the national interest of the United States.

Implicit in the classification of programs and personnel was the assumption that at a particular moment any overseas program could be placed somewhere in the spectrum between programs having a foreign affairs purpose and impact and those having a domestic affairs purpose and impact. If this were the only factor to be taken into account in classifying a program, the problem would be difficult enough. But, in view of the tremendous impact upon both domestic and international affairs of the results of a successful space flight, perhaps even the category into which the station managers and the technical representatives of the National Aeronautics and Space Administration (NASA) fall is open to question. Furthermore, there are the practical considerations of determining which personnel need diplomatic status in the conduct of their duties and which personnel actually receive it in a given country overseas.

Frankly, it must be recognized that there are many gray areas that pose problems of delimitation. The purposes and impact of programs may shift over a period of time and may be or become divergent rather than congruent. Programs included or excluded from attache services may also shift because of external factors that are beyond the full control of the United States. Nonetheless, for administrative purposes experience may serve as a guide to individual decisions. In view of the complexities and variables involved, classification of programs and personnel must be carefully and continuously examined by the participating domestic and foreign affairs agencies and by the Civil Service Commission and the Foreign Service of the United States, with strong support and assistance from the Bureau of the Budget and the Department of State.

NON-ATTACHE-TYPE PROGRAMS AND PERSONNEL

On the basis of the primary function or functions performed by their personnel, twelve overseas programs of the federal domestic agencies were classified in the preceding chapter as being of a non-attache nature. Eight of the twelve carried out regulatory or control duties; three, research duties of one kind or another; and one, administrative and operational functions. By far the greater portion of the non-attache-type personnel overseas are conducting regulatory and control activities that are essentially the extension of a domestic program overseas. The primary purpose of the extension overseas is to make domestic regulation and control more efficient. Clearly the personnel engaged in the three research activities were conducting overseas programs to assist in gaining knowledge of benefit to domestic programs of the agencies concerned. It is true that the impact of the P.L. 480 foreign research programs may also have a side benefit for foreign countries or have a long-range impact on foreign affairs.

Essentially, NASA's station managers and technical representatives are servicing a domestic program that by its very nature must be conducted beyond the boundaries of the United States. Their work, however, is primarily to serve the domestic purposes of the program, and only peripherally are they engaged in public relations activities normally thought of as being performed overseas by representatives of USIA.

While there are personnel problems involved in staffing these non-attache-type overseas programs, none is of such an overriding character as to force the programs to institute other personnel systems. Instead, it is presumed that their emerging needs will be recognized and can be met within the framework of a Civil Service or an "excepted service"—that is, outside the Civil Service.

This does not mean that the personnel management behind these non-attache-type activities does not require improvement. It is extremely important that they be managed in such a way as to perform their assigned functions effectively within the over-all framework of United States policy. Although several of the personnel "systems" servicing the non-attache-type programs are "excepted services," it is imperative that the Civil Service Commission and the Bureau of the Budget lead all the government agencies concerned in studying the personnel requirements for these programs as well as the needs of the personnel serving the programs.

Among the more important problems that deserve attention are:

(1) *Selection.* Persons who are finally chosen to serve overseas normally enter domestic agencies without an intention of pursuing overseas careers and often lack useful basic preparatory training for service abroad.

(2) *Orientation.* Training programs for overseas service are rather informal in most domestic affairs agencies and are generally conducted under pressure with no time to develop adequate "overseasmanship" capabilities.

(3) *Pay and Prerogatives.* Personnel serving abroad in systems outside the Foreign Service are conscious of discrepancies in financial benefits, immunities, and social acceptance. There should be

greater conformity, although complete similarity is neither likely nor essential.

(4) *Career Development.* Domestic agency personnel who take overseas assignments sometimes endanger their domestic careers by prolonged service abroad.

(5) *In-service Training.* Domestic agency personnel who serve primarily abroad will often need training to maintain their expertise and to meet changing requirements.

(6) *Assignment and Rank.* Assignment problems of overseas personnel during periods of service in the United States which may stem from the fact that the Civil Service does not follow the rank-in-man principle of the Foreign Service [3] need careful consideration and some positive resolution.

(7) *Relationships in the United States.* The domestic affairs agencies have to maintain or establish relationships within the United States that will allow a proper review by the Secretary of State—as principal foreign policy adviser to the President—of their overseas programs, personnel assignments, and budgets.

(8) *Relationships Abroad.* At many overseas posts, problems of co-operation with and acceptance of supervision by the ambassador in behalf of the President and the Secretary of State are not yet fully resolved.

Once it is recognized that certain non-attache-type programs require staffing by a career corps that would rotate between the field and the home office, it should be possible to establish personnel provisions that would make such careers more desirable and would attract well-qualified personnel. Participation in similar overseas programs would probably be viewed as a one-time affair, with personnel selected for broadening experience overseas and then returned to the main line of career development within the United States. Increasing permissiveness in Civil Service legislation might be required if the Civil Service Commission is to meet with sufficient flexibility the varying overseas personnel needs of the domestic affairs agencies it serves.

ATTACHE-TYPE PROGRAMS AND PERSONNEL

In brief, attache-type programs require personnel who perform reporting, negotiating, and representational functions in specialized fields. Based on the duties of typical attache-type personnel surveyed in this study, attaches are most likely to perform one or more of the following three functions:

(1) Specialized reporting and negotiation to assist in the formulation of United States foreign policy.

---

[3] See page 16.

(2) Specialized reporting and negotiation necessary to adapt domestic programs and viewpoints to overseas developments in the interests of long-range national security.

(3) Communication with the specialized functional sections of foreign governments and agencies for the exchange of information on developments and governmental positions in the specialized fields.

Increasingly, in recent years, as federal domestic agencies have expanded their overseas interests or as other United States government programs overseas have been terminated or reduced, attaches have performed one or both of two additional functions:

(1) Advice and assistance to United States ambassadors in the monitoring of specialized programs conducted overseas for domestic purposes but which often have foreign policy implications regardless of their stated goals. (Such specialized programs are often carried out by American personnel or local employees who are neither members of the Foreign Service of the United States nor in the service of or under direct hire by any of the foreign affairs agencies.)

(2) Unofficial advice to administrators of programs of foreign governments when such advice is requested and is in the United States national interest. (For example, in a country in which an AID program was terminated or seriously reduced in size, such services would be rendered if the United States had a continuing interest in the success of the "institutions" created with American assistance.)

Another somewhat different function which has come to be accepted is that of trade promotion or guidance in the development of programs that would benefit American business, labor, agricultural, industrial, financial, economic, educational, social, or professional interests. Although several federal domestic agencies have questioned whether this is a proper attache function, they have been more concerned with whether the attache can do a better job of trade promotion within or outside the Foreign Service.

A number of the federal domestic agencies have felt at times and under certain circumstances that their trade promotion or other overseas needs had not been suitably serviced by Foreign Service personnel. Criticism was directed at the number of officers assigned to perform their functions, the level of skill or maturity of these officers, and the degree of interest of the officers in performing their tasks. These criticisms stemmed from the belief that personnel in the Foreign Service traditionally have recognized a primary obligation to the Department of State and not to the domestic agencies they have served temporarily; that promotions and success in their career did not really depend upon the domestic agencies; and that, if they were to reach the top levels of the Foreign Service, they would not be able to focus their interests for long on such mundane problems as trade promotion or other specialized activities.

What could be done on trade promotion or other activities of the federal domestic agencies hinged upon the funds obtained by the Department of State for personnel to conduct these activities from the appropriations subcommittees which normally handled the Department of State budget. In its recruitment and selection processes, the State Department was more interested in securing officers who could become top political-economic generalists than in finding promising trade promotion or other specialized personnel. Career patterns and in-service training were geared to producing generalist officers rather than to creating trade promotion or other specialists of interest to the domestic agencies. Assignment policies tended to rotate Foreign Service officers in a variety of countries and in functional tasks in preparing them as generalists; the federal domestic agencies had little control over which officers were assigned to perform the overseas tasks of interest to them. Foreign Service officers who tended to specialize in trade activities or other domestic agency interests had limited opportunities for advancement within the Foreign Service, although at their levels they received the pay, privileges, fringe benefits, and status accorded other Foreign Service officers of the same rank.

On occasion, this "rather unhappy state of affairs" for the federal domestic agencies was remedied by Congressional action, which permitted the separation from the Foreign Service of overseas representatives serving the trade promotion or other interests of a particular domestic agency, thus giving to an individual federal domestic agency authorization to provide for its own representation abroad. This action set other problems in motion. For example, the Department of State, under these conditions, received reports for policy and negotiating purposes which in a sense were second hand. In certain special fields they were prepared by personnel who were responsible and loyal to another department, whose budgets were obtained from sources not directly influenced by State, and whose original recruitment and selection had been made not on the basis of possible overseas service but rather on the basis of duty in the United States. Career patterns and in-service training were usually controlled by the other departments. The specialists produced had a narrower view of foreign policy than did Foreign Service officers and perhaps related their work more to the needs of their own departments than to the needs of the Department of State. While the State Department and certain ambassadors maintained some control over who would be acceptable at posts abroad and over removal from assignments for cause, assignments tended to be made by the individual federal domestic agencies in their own best interests. For the personnel of the federal domestic agencies serving overseas in separate personnel systems, pay, privileges, fringe benefits, and status in the diplomatic community abroad were usually below that for the Foreign Service officers with whom they worked.

These are the problems that must be confronted and resolved in considering future possible alternative relationships of personnel systems servicing the attache-type functions of interest both to the federal domestic agencies and to the Department of State.

V | ALTERNATIVE ATTACHE RELATIONSHIPS FOR THE FUTURE

(I) COMPLETE INTEGRATION

MOST ATTACHE DUTIES OF INTEREST to domestic agencies are performed by Foreign Service officers and Foreign Service Reserve officers. The standard illustration of an attache function integrated closely with the Foreign Service is the work performed by labor attaches. These attaches are Foreign Service employees of the Department of State, but the Department of Labor has an important voice in personnel actions affecting them. The Department of Labor is consulted on assignments of Foreign Service officers who specialize in international labor matters, is represented as an observer on the Foreign Service boards that consider their promotions, and provides specialized training for them in labor affairs. The Department of Labor also nominates personnel to the Department of State for temporary assignment abroad as Foreign Service Reserve officers with international labor functions. Variations of this type of relationship are illustrated by the civil aviation attaches, who perform work of special interest to the Federal Aviation Agency, and minerals attaches, who are somewhat similarly related to the Department of Interior.

Good reasons can be given to support the use by all attache services of the integrated relationship of personnel performing the labor attache function. Foreign Service career officers trained in observing and reporting on many aspects of the foreign scene and in dealing with people abroad in many specialized fields have traditionally fulfilled the reporting requirements for most government agencies overseas. There is a growing recognition of the need for these Foreign Service officers to specialize in functional or area fields during a portion of their careers. Foreign Service officers so specialized still have a broad background and can relate incidents in specific functional fields to the broader national interest. These Foreign Service officers have been successfully "retreaded" for labor reporting and have displayed an interest in their work.

The Labor Department has been allowed sufficient voice on personnel matters related to the labor area. Foreign Service Reserve officers selected from the Labor Department or the labor movement have had opportunities for broadening their experience and for promotion to top posts within the Foreign Service. Communications with the field between the Labor Department and labor attaches or labor reporting officers are also considered reasonably adequate.

Some Labor Department officials fear that any move away from close integration would attract less qualified personnel to the labor specialty, for labor attaches and labor reporting officers might consequently be excluded from work in the political area which has made the labor specialization particularly attractive.

On the other hand, underlying difficulties in the Labor Department's relationship to the Foreign Service are at present minimized by favorable personal relationships which do not rest on a firm organizational base. Furthermore, neither the Department of Commerce, since its new agreement with the State Department, nor the Departments of Agriculture and Treasury, which now have separate services, would be likely to accept complete integration.

In the past the Labor Department has been content to be primarily a service organization, providing technical support for the Department of State. It has usually bowed to State Department wishes whenever there has been a conflict of interests. But the Labor Department's interest in labor-economic reporting and research is expanding, and it appears unlikely that such increasingly specialized needs can be met successfully in the future by retreaded Foreign Service officers. At present the only course open to Labor Department specialists who wish to advance to the top of the Foreign Service career ladder is for them to enter the Foreign Service at FSO-3 or FSO-2 levels. As its needs grow the Labor Department may become less tolerant of losing its specialists into the general stream of the Foreign Service in this way.

There is little evidence that many of the best officers in the

Foreign Service have been drawn into the labor attache or labor reporting field. With the close relationship of labor and political affairs in many countries overseas, Foreign Service officers are drawn into the labor specialization from consular or other assignments as a stepping stone toward political or economic assignments. Foreign Service Reserve officers performing labor functions are not always "accepted" by Foreign Service officers, partly because they have received too little orientation and have sometimes not been examined or selected in an orderly way. Many Reserve officers lack language training. Too many labor attaches and labor reporting officers are on Washington assignments in the Department of State, and too few are returned to or want to return to the Department of Labor to keep them up to date on labor developments in the United States. Some feel that the Labor Department has not been able to provide sufficient information while they are overseas. The Labor Department, however, may feel less responsibility for the performance of the labor function because of the degree of integration within the Foreign Service.

Specialists in an integrated service, as in the case of some officers performing civil aviation reporting duties, do not want to become experts in only one field for fear of being tabbed as specialists and losing the opportunity for assignment to the "prestige" duties which fall to Foreign Service officers. It is occasionally charged that complete integration in the Foreign Service has reduced the level of competence in specialties so that the Foreign Service cannot match the competence to be found among employees of the federal domestic agencies. Some individuals in the Federal Aviation Agency believe that personnel assigned within the integrated service to observe civil aviation developments lack the degree of specialization that would allow them to evaluate properly what they see and hear abroad in order to write useful reports.

Lack of specialized competence in an integrated Foreign Service would deny to the ambassador the specialized knowledge and advice which he requires if he is to be responsible for American activities in his country and if he is to be able to assist the Secretary of State, as principal foreign policy adviser to the President, in monitoring domestic overseas operations in the national interest.

(2) COMPLETE SEPARATION

A major alternative relationship is found in the separate foreign services maintained by the Departments of Agriculture and the Treasury. Their overseas personnel, though subject to the over-all direction of the United States ambassador in each country, are not members of the Foreign Service of the United States. They receive their instructions from and report to their parent agencies in Washington. Treasury and agricultural attaches represent the United States in dealing with foreign governments and are accorded diplomatic status, but they are employed under the Civil Service personnel system.

The case for separating additional attache services from the Foreign Service of the United States gains strength from the general satisfaction of the Department of Agriculture and the Department of the Treasury with their separate services. They are reasonably happy with their present relationships, see no immediate reason for disturbing the status quo, and feel that their personnel cooperate and fit into the country team at posts abroad.

Representatives of both agencies note the small size of their attache services and their ability to treat members of their overseas staffs as individuals. The possibility of service overseas or in the United States provides a flexibility that is attractive to new recruits who are not definitely committed to one pattern or the other. It seems unlikely that many recruits attracted to the Agriculture and Treasury Departments under current procedures would also be interested in the Foreign Service where they might be given administrative or consular assignments.

Both agencies fear that if they participate in an integrated service arrangement their best people will be drawn off into the broader fields. Because of the traditional importance of the political field in the Foreign Service, agricultural and financial specialists might try to obtain assignments in that field, rather than perform their agricultural and financial specialties to the best of their abilities.

The departments also call attention to what "Wristonization" [1] has done to specialization in the Foreign Service. Only through a close relationship with a domestic affairs agency, they maintain, can specialists attain and retain a deep understanding of a specialized field related to the interests of a domestic agency.

It is believed that a person with working experience in a unit in which reports are received and used does a better reporting job than a

---

[1] The term "Wristonization" is derived from the name of the Chairman of the Public Committee on Personnel, Henry M. Wriston. The Committee, established in 1954 by the Secretary of State, recommended the integration of State Department and Foreign Service personnel. "Wristonees," who were Department officers formerly in the Civil Service and assigned only to Washington posts, became subject to assignment overseas. Positions in the Department were opened to Foreign Service officers. While this flexibility of assignment solved some problems, it created others, such as a loss of specialization by many Wristonees that the Foreign Service officers assigned to Washington could not fill. For an analysis of the effects of Wristonization, see John E. Harr, *The Development of Careers in the Foreign Service,* Foreign Affairs Personnel Studies No. 3 (New York: Carnegie Endowment for International Peace, 1965).

person lacking such experience. An individual with overseas experience serving in a domestic affairs agency can make better use of reports from abroad than those who have never served abroad. He is aware of what went into the preparation of such reports and knows their strengths and weaknesses. Also, personnel in a domestic department who have served overseas in a separate personnel system are more acceptable spokesmen for overseas needs than officers from a "State Department-controlled" integrated Foreign Service.

Department of Agriculture representatives have complained that during the period the Department of Agriculture was associated with the Foreign Service, agricultural attaches were cut disproportionately because of their low priority in an integrated Foreign Service when the Foreign Service suffered budget cuts. Functioning separately, the Department has been able to upgrade its representation and restore its numbers without expanding beyond reason.

Treasury personnel note that in conferences with representatives of the United Kingdom and Canada which have attache systems in which treasury representatives and those of other domestic agencies are not members of the diplomatic service, these representatives often hold more unified policy positions than United States representatives who are members of an integrated Foreign Service.

The Agriculture and Treasury Departments value the fact that their representatives are in a sense outside the embassy hierarchy and can talk directly to the ambassador without going through intermediaries. Both agencies assert that they have been able to maintain the ratings of their overseas personnel when they return for department assignments, even though the rank-in-man principle does not apply within the Civil Service.

While the reasons for separating additional attache services from the Foreign Service seem to have merit, the arguments against separation are extremely strong. For instance, administrators from both departments indicate that at present they are having some difficulty in recruiting well-qualified young people and that many domestic personnel are not interested in temporary assignments overseas. Personnel from the separate services are rarely assigned to high-ranking diplomatic posts. In addition, the services are compelled to apply Civil Service salary scales, which stop at a lower level than the Foreign Service scale. In the past the Treasury Department feared that if it relinquished its separate service its specialists might decide that their careers could be advanced by leaving the Treasury and accepting political assignments within the Foreign Service. However, in this respect, the maintenance of a separate service has not benefited the

Treasury, which is now witnessing the draining off of its top personnel to other agencies, business, and even educational institutions.

Differences in retirement age and benefits, in the timing of salary increases within a grade, in entry duties on personal items such as automobiles, as well as in salary and status limitations resulting from the system of separate services make service overseas less attractive than it would be if some form of attachment to the Foreign Service were worked out which would include these benefits.

Neither agency has been consistently aware of the importance of language and area training for all its personnel embarking on overseas careers, and it appears they lack staffing and orientation patterns that would allow their personnel to meet present standards of the Foreign Service for overseas assignments.

Personnel in these agencies are not subject to assignment abroad in the interests of the agency or nation and can refuse posts that are not of immediate interest to them. Middle-level employees are not anxious to break employment patterns for duty anywhere overseas when they are moving satisfactorily up the domestic career ladder and have established roots and useful contacts in Washington. Although personnel in the Agriculture and Treasury Departments hesitate to admit it, overseas service in their separate foreign services develops different skills than does domestic service and may hinder the domestic career of an officer who has served abroad. The fact that higher rank personnel in the Agriculture Department are sometimes brought back from overseas to fulfill administrative duties rather than more specialized tasks leaves the separated system open to the same charge as the integrated system: failure to preserve the opportunity for individuals to pursue a specialization throughout a career.

Within federal domestic agencies that do not now have separate foreign services, the argument for complete separation normally comes from personnel with new program responsibilities overseas, and in some cases from personnel who have had little or no recent experience in working with or maintaining liaison with the Foreign Service. In these domestic agencies, the argument for separation is often based on a belief that either domestic agencies should have policy responsibilities for their overseas operations, or, at the very least, once policy is decided, the operators should be allowed to operate with minimal or no supervision from the policy-setting agencies.

Those who ardently support less supervision by the Secretary of State argue that ambassadors would eventually run miniature executive branches and the voice of agencies with domestic responsibilities and separate attache services would be heard with perhaps as much force as are their secretaries in Washington. The same persons also believe that the strengthening of the role of domestic agencies overseas would require the creation of a powerful new figure in the Executive Office of the President who would assume the broad advisory duties on overseas programs presently vested in the Secretary of State.

Decisions on personnel reorganization should be formulated in such a way as to upset as little as possible the existing structure. Such judgments should be oriented toward indicating how the present system could be made to work more effectively. The solution then is not to eliminate the broad responsibilities of the Secretary of State. And separation of all attache staffs from the Foreign Service overseas and their control by separate agencies are not steps calculated to strengthen the Secretary of State's ability to serve as an enlightened principal foreign policy adviser to the President.

It appears that specialized personnel from narrow departmental backgrounds would be less able to understand other departments' responsibilities or needs, or to make a contribution to policy synthesis than would personnel serving in a more unified system who had some training experiences in common and had an opportunity for broader service experience during their careers. It may be true that a system of separate attache services that would work for a government of party or ministerial responsibility is a departmental luxury which the United States cannot afford under the American constitutional system of separation of powers.

EXTENSION OF THE STATE-COMMERCE AGREEMENT

The extension of the State-Commerce Agreement to include a number of attache specializations within the Foreign Service is a third possible alternative relationship. Under the terms of the Memorandum of Agreement of November 15, 1961, the Department of Commerce has a formal voice in decisions concerning the recruitment, examination, selection, assignment, training, and promotion of commercial specialists in the Foreign Service. The Agreement provides for formal recognition of the commercial specialization as one of the options in the written entrance examination and as one of the functional specialties that Foreign Service officers can follow on a career basis; it also gives the Department of Commerce budgetary responsibility for the commercial specialization of the Foreign Service, subject to review and concurrence of the Department of State. The budgetary aspect of the Agreement is discussed separately.

The arguments in support of extending the State-Commerce Agreement to include a number of attache specializations within the Foreign Service are compelling. Such a development would involve increased representation and participation by domestic agencies in Foreign Service matters and would provide for both the necessary differences and compatible practices in specialized career tracks within the Foreign Service. It would represent a practical adjustment to political realities. As one observer in the Department of Commerce has put it in referring to the Agreement, "Each department got about 85 per cent of what it wanted, and that's a good agreement."

Since the overseas interests of powerful domestic agencies are continuing to grow, it would appear better, from the viewpoint of achieving policy coordination, to give them an increased voice and greater participation in the management of the Foreign Service than to allow them to set up separate attache services. The extension of provisions analogous to those of the State-Commerce Agreement and adjusted to the needs of the individual agencies would make possible the development of personnel with the qualities needed for synthesizing competing policy interests of federal agencies overseas. By increasing the responsibilities of the domestic agencies within the Foreign Service, the agencies would undoubtedly show a greater interest in keeping specialists up to date in their particular fields.

Recognition of promotion possibilities for specialists to top ranks and titles would allow them to maintain their specialties throughout their careers without the necessity of becoming "generalists" and losing their specializations. The presence of such specialists in a new kind of Foreign Service would help the ambassador to monitor adequately the programs of domestic agencies overseas. The ambassador would be aided by personnel who would be loyal to a service. They would understand not only the broad purpose of such a service but also the needs of some of the specialties within it. If the domestic agencies have not always recognized the importance of language effectiveness or of developing an understanding of foreign political, economic, and social environments, certainly the association of the domestic agencies with the Department of State in a service in which both have an interest is likely to improve the preparation of specialists for overseas assignments. If the Department of State has often appeared to feel that Foreign Service officers could perform any specialty with little training, the closer association may lead to a better understanding of the value of deeper specialization in an increasingly complex world with problems that do not yield to simple solutions. Once specialization is recognized, it will be easier to adjust rotation patterns to the needs of a particular specialization, both as to length of service and to location of assignment.

Participation in recruitment by the departments interested in specialties perhaps for the first time will attract young people with an interest in specialization to take the Foreign Service examination. The Foreign Service has always placed great emphasis on the political field as the one area most likely to lead to promotion in rank and title. This orientation may be somewhat less true in a service with specialized ladders, examinations with special options, and recruitment of individuals with specialized interests.

Relatively narrow specializations that might not hold interest for personnel throughout a career could be made tolerable by assignment in related fields without losing the degree of specialization necessary to the performance of the original specialty. High performance ratings and promotions in the specialized fields would be likely to go to those individuals who were best able to accommodate the concern of an agency with the broader national interests.

Small separate services have been limited in flexibility by their staffing needs. It is likely that participation on a specialized basis in a broader service may give specialists greater career opportunities and allow agencies more flexibility in staffing. Since the career ladders would be somewhat separate and the numbers in each category relatively small, there is little reason to fear that personnel would be merely file numbers who would be dealt with on an impersonal basis.

A specialist in a Foreign Service which allows domestic agencies to participate in its management would be a much more effective representative of foreign policy interests when on assignment in a domestic affairs agency than the specialist from a service dominated by the Department of State. The negotiated character of the new relationship to be set up between the individual domestic agencies and the Foreign Service makes it possible to recognize the individual differences in requirements in order to make each specialty effective.

Such a service would make it possible for domestic affairs agencies to staff and operate many domestic purpose overseas programs with competent specialists. The programs would be under a more enlightened foreign policy control by the ambassador, who would have the assistance of specialized members of his country team, and would be subject to coordination by the State Department, which would also draw on better trained specialists than in the past.

A few thoughtful arguments have been raised against extension of the State-Commerce Agreement. There is the fear that loyalties of specialists in such a Foreign Service would be divided between the domestic agencies and the Department of State rather than synthesized positively in the national interest. Moreover, why should the separate services of the Departments of Agriculture and the Treasury be disturbed when they are presently functioning relatively satisfactorily? Commercial officers in the Foreign Service are worried lest entry into the specialized program cut them off from general economic work which they have found interesting and broadening and which they believe has been helpful in improving the quality of performance of their commercial reporting and policy advisory functions. There is also the belief that more interesting and flexible career patterns are possible in a specialty if an officer is placed in a separate service more closely related to a domestic department. There is less overseas service and greater opportunity to move into a wider variety of departmental positions. Another worry concerns the creation of narrow specialized career ladders. There is some question that even a good recruitment program might not be able to recruit a sufficient number of interested and able young people to fill the staff requirements of specialized programs on a Foreign Service career basis.

The implementation of the Agreement between the Department of State and the Department of Commerce has not yet been worked out in detail, and many areas of hidden disagreement remain to be resolved. Personnel administrators might be inflexible and consequently might try to force all the specializations into a common organizational pattern, even though the negotiated nature of the Agreement should allow for differences in order to make the individual specializations effective.

A more serious question is to what degree the new organization can throw off tradition and past relationships. Can the institution of the Foreign Service actually make the changes called for, not only in structure but also in feelings and in human relationships? Can cooperative patterns be built where separation or domination once existed? Will the lag in adjusting to and using the new relationship be so great as to cause it to fail before there can be any development from a mere ideal to practical reality?

Although the responsibility for budgeting for the commercial specialization program was allocated to the Department of Commerce under the State-Commerce Agreement, there was much less support for the provision than expected. The primary purpose of the provision, it was pointed out, was to find a means of getting larger financial support for the attache services by allowing individual departments or agencies to go for their requests to the Representatives in Congress with whom they were accustomed to working.

The State Department did not believe that it would lose any vital control over the commercial specialization as a result of the budget shift, since the funds were to be reimbursed to State and lost in the general budget. It is possible that the provision was accepted by the

State Department to allow the domestic agencies to discover that it was more difficult than they had thought to get funds to support the attache services—so long as the State Department shielded them from this endeavor and carried the budget responsibility.

Arguments against the original budget provision of the Agreement were not difficult to find. For example, if greater support for attache services were to be obtained through separate budgeting by domestic agencies, it was possible that the State Department's own appropriations would be cut in proportion to its gains from other sources. The prospect of having to assume budget responsibilities worried at least one agency; its appropriations subcommittees were considered so parochial on foreign affairs matters that the budget appropriation was more likely to be cut than to be increased.

There was general concern in the Bureau of the Budget that the shift in budget control was an over-reaction to the need to shift greater responsibility to the domestic agencies directly interested in Foreign Service specializations. Even in the Department of Commerce, responsible officials expressed the belief that since the Department of State had shown its willingness to have the Commerce Department prepare the budget and request the appropriations, it was no longer necessary that this actually be done. The interest of the domestic agencies was not so much in "control" as in achieving a greater degree of consultation with and cooperation among the interested parties.

Several individuals worried about what would happen if certain agencies were able to secure greater support for their attache activities than could others, thereby destroying program balance as well as compatibility of living and working conditions within the embassy community. There was support for a consolidated budget which the Department of State, in full consultation with the departments concerned, could adjust to meet the total requirements of the United States government for attache services overseas.

Smaller separate budgets, which often fluctuate in size, would make it difficult to adjust staffing patterns if severe cuts were imposed. Furthermore, the domestic agencies have supporters in Congress who are less international minded than those of the foreign affairs agencies. Or a domestic agency might not be in the good graces of a particular subcommittee at the time its appropriations for the attache service were being considered and as a consequence might lose most of its appropriations for such purposes.

The Bureau of the Budget's position was that if there were individual agency budget control of attache services along with joint participation in recruitment, examination, assignment, and promotion, in a system where organizational patterns already tended to spread responsibility, the mere fact that people were in the Foreign Service of the United States would not be a sufficiently unifying force to assure any real degree of loyalty to the ambassador or to the Secretary of State. There would be so many divided loyalties and responsibilities and so many concurrences required that effective management would be impeded. Some Budget Bureau officials believed that the personnel in such a system would be more loyal to the individual departments than to the ambassador, the Secretary of State, or the Foreign Service.

CONTINUING THE PRESENT DIVERSE RELATIONSHIPS

Those who want to continue the separate relationship of attache services to the Foreign Service declare that a unified arrangement was not able to provide the degree of specialization now required in United States embassies or now required in the formulation of foreign and domestic policy in Washington. There are differences in the overseas interests of each individual agency; these can best be met by allowing each agency to choose its own relationship to the Foreign Service. The Department of Labor apparently has interests that closely parallel the political interests of the Foreign Service, and its personnel interests are possibly best served by a close integration with the Foreign Service as it has existed. The Commerce Department also does not want to have the commercial specialization too far removed from economic work in the embassies and so stays within the Foreign Service, although its commercial export interests are different enough from the political interests of the Foreign Service to require additional guarantees of participation in personnel control. On the other hand, the Department of Agriculture's interests are so different and specialized that it can afford to operate separately, relying less on the performance of related functions in the Foreign Service for career development than on opportunities within the Department of Agriculture.

Furthermore, it is said that what *is* represents the facts of life in government—a practical balance growing from a continuing power struggle among the departments and between the departments and Congress. The arrangement is flexible enough to suit the individual needs of each department. If there is a need for greater compatibility in allowances and other prerogatives among United States personnel serving overseas, this can be provided by new legislation without establishing a unified personnel system. And, if there is fear of lack of unity in United States policies and programs overseas, it should

88

be remembered that the personnel system is not the only, and probably not the best, means of achieving such unity. Management has budgetary and organizational devices to accomplish these ends.

If a system of diversity seems to resolve some problems, it fails to confront other problems of greater import that question past practices. The present situation of diversity is viewed as unsound for many reasons. It is difficult for departments or agencies to stand in such different relationships to the Foreign Service of the United States. The Labor and Agriculture Departments are already worried by the higher ranks and titles now available to the Commerce Department as a result of the State-Commerce Agreement. Protection of the Labor Department's personnel interests depends in large measure on personal relationships, without the security of a formal agreement like that between the State and Commerce Departments. The Agriculture Department, which has a separate service despite its desires to be part of the embassy team, may wonder if the Commerce Department, because it operates within the Foreign Service, will be given responsibility for functions that are not clearly within the field of one or the other agency. For the moment, Agriculture's fears appear unjustified; the State Department continues to treat the Agriculture Department fairly, perhaps in the hope that it will return to a closer relationship with the Foreign Service. In the long run, however, Agriculture's fears may prove to be real.

Although there is general recognition of a need for greater depth of specialization in the areas that concern the major domestic departments and agencies of government, the present patterns of personnel organization for staffing abroad neither provide the best specialists for overseas duty nor encourage career specialization. In the Labor Department the career ladder for specialists goes no higher than the FSO-3 level; after that they must broaden their field of interest if they hope for further promotion. In Agriculture, specialists must often give up specialization for administrative positions if they want to hold their rank and at the same time be allowed to serve in Washington as well as overseas.

Within an integrated service, there has been very little department responsibility for the training or maintenance of Foreign Service experts in the field of interest of the department. As a result, department resources have not been sufficiently utilized. On the other hand, with separate services, department responsibilities have been so complete that it has been difficult to arrange broadening experiences for department personnel or to give sufficient attention to preparing the specialists for overseas posts.

Within an integrated service, many Foreign Service officers in the labor field who return to Washington for assignments in the Department of State probably do not have a fundamental understanding of the Department of Labor and its needs. By the same token, when agricultural attaches return to Washington for assignment, they almost invariably go to the Department of Agriculture and are not available for assignment to the Department of State to give the advantage of their specialized advice to the Secretary of State.

If the domestic agencies are to expand their activities overseas, and if the ambassador is, in fact, to be responsible for all United States operations within his country, each ambassador will need specialized advice from members of the attache services. Foreign Service officers in an integrated service without sufficient experience in domestic affairs agencies are not normally in a position to monitor domestic programs overseas adequately in behalf of the ambassador. Officers in a separate service of a domestic department can hardly judge their own department's case for the ambassador.

Not the least advantage of a more cooperative relationship of all attache services within the Foreign Service concerns the budget and appropriation process. If the services are separate and each agency obtains its appropriations from its own special subcommittees of the Congress, there can be no fully rational and balanced surveillance of country programs by Congress. Furthermore, since each agency's budget is processed through separate sections of the Bureau of the Budget, if services are separate it is difficult for the Executive Branch to obtain a broad view of the balance in attache services in a country. It is true that the embassy has a responsibility to present a balanced country program, but it is evident that this responsibility is not met evenly by all ambassadors. Central budgeting in the State Department for specialized attache services within the Foreign Service, with full consultation of the individual interested participants, would substantially reduce these difficulties. Review by the foreign affairs agencies of all domestic affairs agency budgets for programs overseas would further help to develop coordinated programs in individual countries.

It is true that a personnel system is not the only means of establishing a degree of unity in services abroad, but it is not unrelated to the achievement of this goal. It might also be the basis for improving agency cooperation in Washington. If properly organized, a personnel system might lead to a synthesis of policy in the national interest rather than stimulating division and conflict among competing departments.

APPENDIX A

Excerpt from Report
of the Committee
on Foreign Affairs Personnel *

Recommendation 11

The Foreign Service of the United States should, as a general rule, serve as the vehicle for those overseas activities of the other agencies of the Government which, though primarily domestic, have an important bearing on foreign policy; for this purpose, its personnel administration should be modified to accommodate better the needs and interests of those agencies. If it should be necessary to make an exception for a large overseas program of such a domestic agency, its overseas personnel should constitute a member of the family of foreign affairs services.

As emphasized in Chapter II of this report, the Department of State has a proper concern in all overseas activities with significant foreign policy implications. It is essential that these activities be carried out within the framework of United States foreign policy objectives and country program plans and that overseas representatives of the various agencies speak with one voice. Other executive departments and agencies of the Government, however, have statutory responsibilities which require overseas representation, and which also have a bearing on the achievement of foreign policy objectives. In short, there is a legitimate duality of interests.

The Committee is convinced that, in the context of the new diplomacy, further proliferation of separate foreign services by domestic agencies would jeopardize the responsibility of the Secretary of State in guiding our foreign policy. It believes that the arrangement best calculated to achieve a desirable balance is one in which overseas personnel engaged in such activities are members of the Foreign Service of the United States, provided, however, that: (1) the personnel management of the Foreign Service is modified to accommodate the specialized overseas interests of the domestic agencies concerned; and (2) these agencies are assured a substantial voice in decisions affecting personnel assigned to perform work in their behalf.

More specifically, the Committee recommends the following guiding principles for the conduct of overseas activities of domestic agencies with a significant relationship to United States foreign policy and its execution:

1. The establishment of new foreign affairs services abroad leading to the further proliferation of personnel systems among the various departments and agencies of the Government should be avoided.

2. With respect to overseas activities now carried out by the Foreign Service of the United States in behalf of other domestic agencies, these agencies should participate in decisions affecting personnel assigned to perform such work, but full budgetary and financial responsibility should be vested in the Department of State. The Committee sees no reason to permit the creation of overseas personnel systems by the departments and agencies now developing new program interests abroad and urges that efforts be made to accommodate them within the Foreign Service of the United States.

3. The Foreign Service personnel system should be so modified with respect to recruitment, examination, selection, training, assignments, and promotions, as recommended elsewhere in this report, as to accommodate the specialized overseas interests of domestic agencies.

4. If the arrangements and modifications referred to above prove successful, consideration should at a later date be given to bringing into the Foreign Service of the United States the overseas personnel of the Foreign Agricultural Service of the Department of Agriculture and the Treasury representatives or attachés of the Department of the Treasury.

5. Whatever the arrangement, the Secretary of State should have authority to review and approve or disapprove proposed programs, major assignments, and budgets in every overseas country for all such activities, and the ambassadors should continue to direct and supervise these activities insofar as they affect United States representation and policy.

While the Committee believes that the national interest would best be served by the recommendation outlined above, it also recognizes the practical difficulties, especially in the near future, of applying such a recommendation without exception. If it should prove necessary to permit, for the time being, a separate personnel system for any of the larger overseas programs with a substantial bearing on foreign policy, the Committee recommends that such a system be organized as a member of the proposed family of foreign affairs services.

APPENDIX B

Memorandum of Agreement Between the Department of State and the Department of Commerce on International Commercial Activities, November 15, 1961

PREAMBLE

IN FULFILLING THAT ROLE in the conduct of foreign affairs which is prescribed by the President, the Secretary of State must of necessity take into account the overseas interests of many United States Government agencies. Concomitantly it is incumbent not only upon him, but also upon other United States Government agencies engaged in overseas activities, to enhance to the maximum possible extent the capacity of U. S. Chiefs of Mission to fulfill the broad responsibilities vested in them by the President in his letter of May 29, 1961.

It is agreed that the Secretary of State and the U. S. Chiefs of Mission can most effectively fulfill their responsibilities and represent the overseas interests abroad of U. S. Government agencies by means of a unified Foreign Service operating under the direction and control of the Secretary of State.

In the discharge of his responsibilities the Secretary of State recognizes the need to maximize the flexibility of the unified Foreign Service and thereby increase its capacity to utilize the talents of specialists competent to represent the interests of those Government agencies served by the Foreign Service.

I. OBJECTIVE

The President has directed the Executive Agencies to place maximum emphasis on enlarging the foreign commerce of the United States in seeking to maintain an over-all balance in our international payments. He has charged the Department of Commerce with the leadership within the Government to insure that a vigorous effort be made to expand trade, travel, and investment and "to provide energetic leadership to American industry in a drive to develop export markets." He has called upon the Departments of State and Commerce to proceed jointly to increase commercial representation and facilities abroad. And he has made it clear that Chiefs of Mission shall oversee and coordinate all such activities abroad.

To provide effective leadership, the Department of Commerce is assuming primary responsibility and direction for foreign trade promotion activities at home and abroad, giving due consideration to interests of other agencies.

The Departments of State and Commerce agree that the President's directive can best be carried out abroad by a single overseas service. To fulfill their respective responsibilities, the two Departments undertake to establish new arrangements for the purpose of providing optimum commercial services within the frame-work of a unified Foreign Service.

To this end the Department of State agrees to develop, with the full participation of the Department of Commerce, a Commercial Specialist Program within the Foreign Service.

II. ROLE OF THE DEPARTMENT OF COMMERCE IN INTERNATIONAL ACTIVITIES

The Department of Commerce is responsible for promoting the nation's industry and business, its foreign and domestic commerce, its scientific and technical growth, and a balanced transportation system. The Department helps business and the Government to achieve their mutual aims of full profitable production and full gainful employment. It provides business and Government with information and assistance and it presents the needs of business in the councils of Government and the needs of Government in the councils of business. These functions include both foreign and domestic activity which, in some cases, are so delicately intertwined that it is impossible to separate them.

The Department's principal foreign economic activities center around services to business engaged in international trade, travel, and investment, and participation in the formulation of U. S. foreign economic policy. The Department's role in the first group is predominant; in the second, the Department recognizes the primacy of the Department of State in the field of foreign economic policy and together with other agencies participates in the formulation thereof.

The Department of Commerce will call upon the commercial specialists at Foreign Service posts to fulfill its responsibilities for services to business.

In matters relating to foreign economic policy, the Department of Commerce will rely upon commercial specialists for the information necessary regarding the business interests aspects in this field. In addition, the Department of Commerce will continue to rely to a significant degree upon the economic staffs at Foreign Service posts for the reporting and representation activities that it requires to fulfill its role in the formulation of foreign economic policy. It will continue to consult regularly with the Department of State as to the reporting necessary to meet its needs.

III. ROLE OF THE DEPARTMENT OF STATE

The President has stated that the relationship of trade, aid, and other aspects of foreign economic policies involve the interests of many agencies of Government, particularly when both foreign and domestic economic considerations are an issue. He also has stated it is essential that interagency consultation and coordination be as meaningful and productive as possible and that the Secretary of State become the focal point of responsibility for the coordination of foreign economic policies. As trade and commercial activity is intimately associated with foreign economic policy, the Department of State must of necessity participate in commercial and trade promotional functions abroad. However, it recognizes the primary role of the Department of Commerce in the promotion of trade, travel, and investment.

In order to avoid duplication, the Departments of State and Commerce will rely upon the unified Foreign Service for their respective overseas needs in these closely related activities.

IV. COMMERCIAL SPECIALIST PROGRAM

The Department of State recognizes the need for a Commercial Specialist Program within the Foreign Service in order to buttress the President's Export Expansion Program. To develop such a program within the Foreign Service, the Department of State will (a) identify a group of career commercial specialists from the ranks of Foreign Service Officers; (b) enlarge the number of appointments into the Foreign Service Reserve from the Department of Commerce and the business world; and (c) incorporate these officers into a Commercial Specialist Program.

It shall be the policy of the Department of State to permit Foreign Service Officers who so elect to devote their careers to commercial specialization. This policy will not preclude other assignments from time to time. All Foreign Service Officers will be given an opportunity to elect for a career in commercial specialization. The personnel files of officers who so elect will be so identified. Advancement shall be based on merit as commercial officers and on an officer's standing in relation to other members of his Foreign Service class. For those who qualify, such specialization may lead to positions of the highest responsibility in the Foreign Service, including ambassadorships.

V. BUDGETING FOR FOREIGN SERVICE COMMERCIAL ACTIVITIES

The Department of Commerce will prepare annually an initial estimate of budgetary requirements for the staffing of commercial specialist positions and all related resource needs within the Foreign Service. This estimate will be jointly reviewed by both Departments and, subject to the concurrence of the Department of State, will be incorporated in the budget of the Department of Commerce.

The Department of State and the Department of Commerce will jointly support before the Bureau of the Budget and the Congress the approved estimates for the Commercial Specialist Program within the Foreign Service.

The funds appropriated to the Department of Commerce for the Commercial Specialist Program will be reimbursed to the Department of State for use in support of this Program.

In the allocation or reallocation of appropriated funds, the Department of State will be guided by the recommendations of the Department of Commerce.

VI. PERSONNEL ADMINISTRATION OF FOREIGN SERVICE ACTIVITIES RECRUITMENT

The Department of State in accordance with its current operating principles and procedures and in collaboration with the Department of Commerce will undertake to recruit Foreign Service Officers at class 8 level for later commercial specialization within the Foreign Service.

The Department of State agrees that it will expand its recruiting efforts, including publicity, visits, and related items, to include the graduates of various universities and colleges giving undergraduate and graduate degrees in Business Administration or Foreign Trade. The Department of Commerce agrees, on its part, to provide the Department of State with recommended lists of such universities and colleges and to make available personnel for service on joint recruitment teams visiting these institutions.

The Department of State working with the Department of Commerce will make a study of the written portion of the Foreign Service Officer Examination to determine:

a) That its content measures the competence of graduates in business administration or foreign trade;

b) What additional measures may be taken to attract candidates for the Foreign Service interested in commercial specialization.

The Department of State will develop optional sections in the written portion of the Foreign Service Officer Examination for the benefit of candidates with background and interest in commercial activities. The Department of Commerce will continue to participate with voting rights on oral examining boards.

The Department of Commerce also will continue to recruit businessmen for service abroad as commercial specialists in the Foreign Service Reserve.

Appointment, Assignment, Transfer, and Promotions

The Department of State and the Department of Commerce will continue to work together to strengthen and to encourage commercial specialization in the Foreign Service. In this regard, the Department of State will view commercial specialists as a functional group within the Foreign Service.

The Department of Commerce will recommend to the Department of State employees of the Department of Commerce for appointment as commercial officers in the Foreign Service Reserve. In addition, the

Department of Commerce will be primarily responsible for recommending for such appointment businessmen and other non-governmental personnel possessing suitable background in industry, trade, travel and investment.

In determining the locations of commercial specialist positions within the Foreign Service, the Department of State will be guided by the recommendations of the Department of Commerce. The Department of State agrees to assign and transfer to these positions those officers who have elected to be commercial specialists or have indicated preference for commercial assignments, and who are recommended by the Department of Commerce. The promotion of these specialists will be governed by the precepts and findings of Selection Boards on which the Department of Commerce representative will participate, including voting rights on those Boards mutually agreed upon. The Department of Commerce will also participate in the formulation of said precepts.

The Department of Commerce agrees to increase substantially the number of its substantive and non-training assignments, including those in its Field Offices, to which Foreign Service Officers specializing in commercial work may be assigned on rotation. Foreign Service Officers not specializing in commercial work, may be given special assignments, upon agreement between the two Departments, to these or other positions in the Department of Commerce or to overseas positions designated for commercial specialists.

VII. RESPONSIBILITIES AND DUTIES OF FOREIGN SERVICE COMMERCIAL SPECIALISTS

The responsibilities and duties of commercial specialists are set forth in Attachment A to this agreement.

The Department of Commerce, with the concurrence of the Department of State, will prepare a *Guide for Commercial Officers* containing a detailed, standardized description of duties of commercial specialists and other Foreign Service personnel performing commercial work abroad.

The commercial specialist will be alert to all foreign economic policy matters in which the Department of Commerce has an interest and will participate as appropriate in activities involving such matters.

In the interest of the most efficient servicing of the needs of both Departments, posts may require economic reporting officers to devote a certain amount of their time on activities set forth as responsibilities of commercial specialists. Conversely, it is recognized that commercial specialists may be called upon to devote a certain percentage of their time to economic reporting and representational functions. Such arrangements will be worked out as the need arises.

Chiefs of Mission will be reminded of the contributions that can be made by commercial officers in those deliberations which substantially affect the commercial interests of the United States in or with the country of assignment.

VIII. TRAINING OF FOREIGN SERVICE COMMERCIAL SPECIALISTS AND LOCAL EMPLOYEES

To maximize the talents and capabilities of commercial specialists within the Foreign Service, the Department of State and the Department of Commerce jointly will cooperate to establish in the School of Foreign

Affairs of the Foreign Service Institute a Department of Commercial Affairs. It will be chaired by a mutually acceptable nominee of the Department of Commerce. The chairman, among other responsibilities, will develop the nature and scope of the commercial training program and, upon approval by the Director of the Foreign Service Institute, supervise its implementation and operation.

Commercial specialists will be provided opportunity to participate in the broader training programs of the Foreign Service Institute. Conversely, other Foreign Service Officers may participate in the commercial training program. The Department of Commerce will make provision for rotational training assignments in its headquarters and field offices as well as in business organizations throughout the country.

Both Departments agree that local nationals performing commercial work abroad may be brought to this country on a selective basis for training.

The dimensions of the training program will be concordant with funds provided therefor by the Department of Commerce to the Department of State on a reimbursable basis.

IX. PROCEDURES FOR INSTRUCTING COMMERCIAL SPECIALISTS AND OTHER OFFICERS ENGAGED IN COMMERCIAL WORK

As used in this agreement, the term "Commercial Specialist Program" relates to the responsibilities and duties of commercial specialists set forth in Attachment A to this agreement. Accordingly, the Department of Commerce, with the approval of the Department of State, will normally develop and prepare instructions for carrying out the responsibilities and duties specified in Part I thereof; and the Department of State, in consultation with the Department of Commerce, will make appropriate modifications of basic instructions to the Foreign Service, including the Foreign Affairs Manual and the CERP.

The Foreign Affairs Manual and Department of Commerce procedures shall be amended to insure fuller and faster and, where appropriate, more direct response to trade inquiries, including those inquiries referred to the Department of Commerce for reply.

The CERP will be amended by developing a revised Section A to provide for those special aspects of the present CERP concerning business services and related commercial interests. This section will include *Commercial Specialist Program Reporting*. The Department of Commerce will originate unscheduled or spot instructions under this section as necessary.

Further, with respect to the CERP, pursuant to the Foreign Service Act of 1946, as amended, and Executive Order 10249 of June 4, 1951, the Department of State will continue to be responsible for foreign economic reporting activities on behalf of departments and agencies of the U. S. Government, and will continue to consult with the Department of Commerce and other agencies in fulfilling this responsibility.

To provide a reasonable balance between available staff and resources abroad and business requests at home, the Department of Commerce agrees to be primarily responsible for control over workload of the Commercial Specialist Program, without prejudice to over-all control responsibilities of the Department of State. For this purpose, the Department of Commerce will establish a central point of control as soon as possible.

All communications relating to the Commercial Specialist Program will be identified, processed, reproduced, and transmitted as provided for in Section XII of this agreement. The Department of Commerce will have primary responsibility for action on such communications and will consult with other agencies as appropriate.

Instructions from either Department to officers performing commercial work will be subject to joint clearance when the substance of such instructions has a bearing on the responsibilities of the other Department.

****

Both Departments will renew and intensify their efforts to reduce reporting requirements to a level consistent with their most significant and comprehensive needs in order thereby to free commercial specialists for increased direct trade promotional activities.

X. DIPLOMATIC STATUS, TITLE AND RANK OF COMMERCIAL SPECIALISTS WITHIN THE FOREIGN SERVICE

To enable commercial specialists to carry out abroad the full range of their responsibilities with maximum effectiveness, the Department of State will seek to obtain for them the diplomatic status and corresponding titles consistent with diplomatic practice, the needs of other U. S. agencies, and the Department's responsibilities. Such titles may include that of Minister for Commercial Affairs when appropriate.

In arriving at a judgment as to an appropriate diplomatic status and corresponding title for a commercial specialist, the Department of State will take fully into account the needs and recommendations of the Department of Commerce.

XI. INSPECTION OF COMMERCIAL SPECIALISTS AND FACILITIES WITHIN THE FOREIGN SERVICE

The Foreign Service Inspection Corps will continue to be responsible for the inspection of commercial personnel and facilities within the Foreign Service. However, in view of the increasing importance of commercial operations at Foreign Service posts, wherever possible inspection teams should include Foreign Service Officers experienced in commercial matters. Officers who have elected to become commercial specialists may be appointed as inspectors. The Department of State will continue to consult with the Department of Commerce in the preparation of instructions covering the inspection of commercial activities. The Department of State also will continue to consult with the Department of Commerce to assure that such instructions appropriately reflect the interests of the Department of Commerce in economic matters.

The Department of State will continue to make available to the Department of Commerce, for its use and comment simultaneously with distribution within the Department of State, those portions of inspection reports which concern the commercial and economic operations of Foreign Service posts.

Additionally, the Department of Commerce may find it desirable to send, from time to time, members of its own Department to observe commercial operations at Foreign Service posts with a view to maximizing the effectiveness of these operations. The observations resulting from such visits will be made known to the officers concerned, to the principal officer at the post, and simultaneously to the Departments of State and Commerce.

XII. COMMUNICATIONS PROCEDURES

The Departments of State and Commerce recognize the necessity for expeditious communications between Foreign Service posts and the Department of Commerce. The Department of State agrees, within available resources, to provide and maintain such communications facilities and procedures as will enable the Department of Commerce to fulfill its responsibilities.

A new communications caption will be established by the Department of State for communications regarding the Commercial Specialist Program and for support activities of a commercial nature. Communications to be so designated will be specifically set forth in a chapter of the Foreign Affairs Manual and will be identified by the caption COMMERCIAL PROGRAM. The Department of Commerce will assume responsibility for the processing, reproduction, distribution and maintenance and servicing within its own Department, as well as for other interested Government agencies, of all incoming communications transmitted by pouch and identified by this caption. The two Departments will consult as to when these responsibilities will be assumed by the Department of Commerce. The Department of State will continue to process, reproduce, and distribute within the U. S. Government all telegraphic messages so identified.

In consideration of the Department of State's over-all coordinating responsibility of Foreign Service activities and necessary control of communications and facilities, outgoing COMMERCIAL PROGRAM communications will be signed or initialed in the Department of State for the Secretary. The Department of State will continue to process, reproduce, and distribute within the U. S. Government all outgoing written communications. Incoming non-telegraphic communications captioned COMMERCIAL PROGRAM will be transmitted directly to the Department of Commerce for processing, reproduction, and distribution; the Department of Commerce will be the primary action agency, but will consult with other agencies when appropriate.

Communications not captioned COMMERCIAL PROGRAM but which are of interest to the Department of Commerce, shall continue to be processed, reproduced, and distributed by the Department of State to other agencies to the extent appropriate including assignment of action.

In cases of urgency relating to the COMMERCIAL PROGRAM, commercial communications facilities between the Department of Commerce or its Field Offices and Foreign Service posts abroad may be utilized. The Department of State will be informed by the Department of Commerce or the Foreign Service post, as appropriate, of all such direct communications of substance.

Similar communications facilities may be employed by Foreign Service posts in responding directly to urgent inquiries from American businessmen in the United States or elsewhere. In such cases, informational copies of messages will be furnished to the Department of Commerce.

****

XIX. IMPLEMENTATION OF THE AGREEMENT

The Department of State and the Department of Commerce agree, with the concurrence of the Bureau of the Budget, that this agreement becomes effective upon signature, and will be amended as deemed necessary.

For the Department of State:
(*Signed*) Dean Rusk
Secretary of State

For the Department of Commerce:
(*Signed*) Luther H. Hodges
Secretary of Commerce

ATTACHMENT A

Responsibilities and Duties of Foreign Service Commercial Specialists

PART I: COMMERCIAL PROGRAM RESPONSIBILITIES

The Commercial Specialist is primarily responsible for promoting the overseas trade, travel, and private investment interests of the United States, as set forth below.

A. Operational Responsibilities

1. Conduct the commercial work of the post.

2. Provide the following services for American and local businessmen who request assistance directly from Foreign Service posts:

(a) Give guidance and assistance promptly in finding and establishing business connections.

(b) Provide suitable background information about potential customers, sources of supply or other potential business opportunities.

(c) Assist in preparing and presenting business proposals.

(d) Where appropriate, arrange appointments and assist in contacts with local government officials.

(e) Prepare prompt and responsive replies to trade inquiries.

(f) Furnish other direct assistance as appropriate.

3. Promote exports of American goods and products; develop trade leads and export opportunities for American businessmen and perform follow-up activity; engage in all necessary institutional promotion of American products.

4. Promote private investment and licensing opportunities.

5. Maintain contact with foreign businessmen and government officials for the purpose of promoting American trade, investment and travel interests, and for protection of such interests abroad.

6. Maintain and operate commercial libraries and files of commercial and economic information for use in assisting American and local businessmen.

7. Travel extensively in area of assignment for the purpose of promoting American commercial interests.

8. Make every effort to bring about the use of United States standards and specifications to permit U. S. firms to compete more effectively; make known potential letting of bids and attend bid openings where U. S. firms are involved; gather information on bid practices generally.

9. Encourage participation by U. S. business in local trade fairs and exhibitions and, where feasible, operate trade information centers; provide information and assistance to foreign businessmen and local government officials on trade fairs and exhibitions held in the United States.

10. Take appropriate steps to prevent trade complaints and assist in resolving those that occur.

11. Assist in promotion of travel to the United States.

B. Support of Special Overseas Activities of the Department of Commerce

1. Participate in the planning and execution of the trade mission program and exploit fully the trade opportunities and contacts developed by trade missions.

2. Where Trade Centers are established, provide direction, guidance and substantive support to the trade promotion effort of such Centers.

3. Assist in the development and operation of official U. S. trade exhibitions.

4. Where Travel Offices are established, or travel officers are located, provide appropriate assistance.

5. Assist in the planning and operation of other special overseas activities of the Department of Commerce, such as market and investment survey teams.

C. Reporting

1. Prepare all commercial reports of the post, as set forth in amended Section A of the CERP, *Commercial Specialist Program Reporting,* and as otherwise required by appropriate instructions.

2. As appropriate, provide adequate and timely information on business trends, commercial developments, and laws, regulations, practices, and customs affecting U. S. commercial interests.

3. Participate in post reporting responsibilities as set forth in Part II of this Attachment.

PART II: GENERAL RESPONSIBILITIES

1. Serve as an integral part of the total operation of the post.

2. Participate in the economic work and reporting responsibilities of the post, particularly with respect to:

    (a) pressing for the removal of import and other restrictions and discriminatory treatment which adversely affect U. S. business interests;

    (b) reporting on commercial policies;

    (c) other economic reporting as appropriate.

APPENDIX C

*Notes on Personnel Relations of
Domestic Agencies With the Agency
for International Development*

FACTS AND IDEAS presented here were gathered and developed in the process of a series of interviews designed to obtain an over-all understanding of personnel activities of domestic agencies supporting United States government programs overseas, whether for domestic agency purposes, those of the Department of State, or those of other agencies. Although interviews did not focus on personnel relationships of domestic agencies with AID, a number of individuals interviewed commented on this subject.

THREE TYPES OF PERSONNEL RELATIONSHIPS

AID secures many of its employees by direct hire, and it is possible for an employee of a domestic agency to obtain employment with AID and give up re-employment rights with his original agency. A second procedure is for a domestic agency employee to be transferred to AID for a specific purpose and to retain re-employment rights in the domestic agency, which may be asserted when the transfer purpose has been achieved. In both of these situations, the employees are carried on AID personnel rolls and paid directly by AID.

A third possibility is for personnel to remain on the personnel rolls of the domestic agency while performing services to AID. In this situation, the individuals are under the technical direction of the domestic agency but subject to general supervision and coordination by the United States Operations Mission Director overseas. They are paid by the domestic agency from funds appropriated to AID but transferred to the domestic agency by agreement.

As an example of the second and third relationships, the Bureau of Reclamation in the Department of Interior has about forty persons who have been transferred to AID with re-employment rights. There are also about fifty persons in its own personnel system working for AID on contract, some on a study of the Blue Nile River system and others operating and maintaining a valley project in Afghanistan. In neither instance do employees have rights to "one certain job" if and when they return for an assignment in the Bureau of Reclamation.

JOB REQUIREMENTS

The specializations required on AID assignments appear to be "deeper" than those required in "attache services" related to the Department of State, yet not as deep and somewhat broader than those from which domestic agency specialists who service AID are drawn. Some of the tasks are for projects that require blending the talents of many different kinds of specialists to achieve an over-all result; other projects only call for efforts by one type of specialist for successful results. Some of the projects are long term and have no definite period for conclusion; others can be defined in such a way as to have a clear break-off point. Certain assignments within projects require personnel for long tours of duty; other assignments may require personnel with deep specialization for only a week or for several months.

PRESENT PROBLEMS

As yet, no adequate means have been worked out to provide AID with a trained reserve of personnel who have deep specializations in domestic agencies. It is generally recognized that for duty with AID, domestic agency specialists need "overseasmanship" qualifications not normally required in the performance of their regular domestic jobs.

There is no way of predicting AID's requirements for domestic agency specialists except on a year to year basis. As a result, specialists are asked on an ad hoc basis to interrupt their domestic careers. Personnel requirements for domestic programs are in competition with AID needs, and the "pipeline" period required to develop adequate specialists for these competing demands can be from three to fifteen years.

Even if re-employment rights are promised, overseas service does not always lead to advancement within a specialty for the returning employee (particularly if the service with AID is for a period of more than three years), and promotions given at the time of acceptance of an overseas assignment are sometimes lost upon return. There is little evidence that the domestic agencies are releasing their best specialist personnel for transfer to AID or that these specialists are interested in such transfer.

In some instances the young specialist benefits from service overseas if the experience is drawn to the attention of his superiors. But he also stands to lose by being out of the country when a position opens up for which he is qualified. Moreover, prolonged service tends to destroy the original deep specialization and when the specialist returns from abroad, he is often given assignments requiring less specialization and more administrative ability.

Tours of duty for AID projects cannot be forecast easily. They vary in duration and come up without any warning, so that accepting AID assignments requires a more adventuresome spirit than most specialists can muster. Moreover, the domestic agencies believe that generally AID is not as close as they are to the source of supply for deep specialization, and that therefore AID does not tap fully the resources available outside the government.

AGENCY PROPOSALS FOR MEETING PROBLEMS

Recognizing overseas service as a career. The Department of Labor, for example, has proposed that AID budget for and contract with the Department to provide a pool of labor specialists who would be trained for overseas assignments and would agree to serve either in the United States or abroad. The Federal Aviation Agency has actually taken the first man into a new "career service," the members of which will alternate between domestic and overseas assignments. Such a service might (*a*) increase training in "overseasmanship"; (*b*) increase the number of specialists interested in overseas service by attempting to meet the rank-in-man principle; (*c*) give career personnel a promotion structure that is separate from and not in competition with the domestic arrangement; and (*d*) make provision for retraining and "refueling" specialists.

On the other hand, there are a number of problems that arise: (*a*) certain types of specialists are in demand overseas for relatively short periods; (*b*) AID's over-all level of needs for specialists fluctuates; (*c*) in this kind of service, careers might not be as good as those in the domestic agencies; (*d*) most of the programs are too small for satisfactory career staffing; (*e*) because of the degree of specialization required, selection for such a career service might have to be postponed for three to fifteen years after entry into the personnel system of the domestic agency; and (*f*) the irregularity of tours would be difficult for many individuals to adjust to satisfactorily.

Contracting specific jobs to domestic agencies. An example of this is the river basin planning study conducted for a six-year period by the Bureau of Reclamation in the Department of the Interior under a contract with AID's predecessor agencies.

In support of this recommendation, it is said that: (*a*) giving the responsibility to the individual agencies would encourage them to assign better personnel to AID projects; (*b*) domestic agency personnel would more readily accept assignments within the scope of their own agency's responsibility; (*c*) both the agencies and the domestic agency personnel would strive to do the job well.

On the other hand, the argument against this scheme is that: (*a*) the number of specialists from within the domestic agencies with an interest in overseas service is limited; (*b*) many of those who are interested have not been prepared for overseas jobs, and there is no uniform acceptance of the need for such training, let alone a regular program of adequate orientation prior to overseas assignment; (*c*) there is no assurance that a domestic agency can maintain a staff sufficient to meet the needs of its domestic programs as well as the needs of AID programs, which fluctuate in size and emphasis; and (*d*) AID may have some problem in maintaining central program control if too much responsibility is turned over to individual domestic agencies.

Conclusions. One basic problem has been Congressional reluctance to accept AID as a long-term program. Moreover, there has never been careful projection of the scope and evolving emphasis of such a program.

The Labor Department's proposal to train specialists for possible overseas assignments on a contract or agreed basis with AID has possibilities and should not be rejected out of hand. It is too early to assess the Federal Aviation Agency's attempt to form a "career service," but it is certainly no ready answer to present problems.

In view of the job requirements to be met by AID, it seems likely that staffing will not only have to include a core career staff for AID, which would rotate between the field and the agency, but also a more deeply specialized career staff with normal United States assignments in domestic agencies or under special arrangement in various types of private institutions to refresh and maintain specialization; a small and partially trained reserve which would be called on from time to time to leave domestic agency or private institutional assignments; and, in some instances, personnel from the domestic agencies working under the technical direction of their agencies on contract to perform specific and well-defined tasks. In addition, short-term visits overseas by experts (government or private) requested on an ad hoc consultative basis will sometimes be useful.

It is recognized that AID must have central control of overseas development operations. This can be achieved to a certain degree if AID manages its own personnel system. Furthermore, its operations should be under the general policy direction of the State Department. When domestic affairs agencies provide personnel for AID programs, the personnel will need unified guidance and direction if the objectives of United States policy are to be achieved.